![Fodor's]

Rome's
25Best

by Tim Jepson

Fodor's Travel Publications
New York • Toronto
London • Sydney • Auckland
www.fodors.com

How to Use This Book

This guide is divided into four sections

• Essential Rome: An introduction to the city and tips on making the most of your stay.

• Rome by Area: We've broken the city into six areas, and recommended the best sights, shops, entertainment venues, nightlife and restaurants in each one. Suggested walks help you to explore on foot.

• Where to Stay: The best hotels, whether you're looking for luxury, budget or something in between.

• Need to Know: The info you need to make your trip run smoothly, including getting about by public transport, weather tips, emergency phone numbers and useful websites.

Navigation In the Rome by Area chapter, we've given each area its own tint, which is also used on the locator maps throughout the book and the map on the inside front cover.

Maps The fold-out map accompanying this book is a comprehensive street plan of Rome. The grid on this fold-out map is the same as the grid on the locator maps within the book. We've given grid references within the book for each sight and listing.

Contents

Introducing Rome

Rome is one of the world's great cities, the city of the Caesars, of romance and *la dolce vita*, of long, hot sunny days, of endless art galleries, churches and museums, of fountain-splashed piazzas and majestic monuments to its golden age of empire.

It is also a city with all the myriad pleasures of any Italian destination—notably superb food and wine—as well as great bars, cafés, and shopping, vibrant nightlife and numerous cultural events. At the same time, Rome is very much a contemporary city—traffic rumbles around medieval cobbled streets and the skyline bristles not with glittering skyscrapers but with the domes of churches and palaces.

But how to visit a city where there is so much to see? First of all don't rush to the Colosseum, St. Peter's or the Sistine Chapel on your first morning. Rome for much of the year is hot and crowded. If you try to cram in too much, or soldier on through the heat, the chances are you'll emerge battered rather than enraptured. Instead, start with a stroll around the Ghetto or Trastevere, two of the city's quaintest old quarters, or

have a cappuccino in one of Rome's loveliest squares, Campo de' Fiori or Piazza Navona. Or maybe head for one of the lesser-known art-filled churches, such as Santa Maria del Popolo, crammed with masterpieces by Raphael, Pinturicchio and Caravaggio.

Once gently acclimatized, and hopefully charmed by the city's quieter side, then you can begin to think about the Trevi Fountain, the Spanish Steps, the Roman Forum or the Vatican Museums. And, of course, the newer but still relatively unsung museums that have opened in the last decade—notably the Palazzo Altemps and Palazzo Massimo alle Terme. But bear in mind this is a living city with more than 3,000 years of history. One, two, even ten visits aren't enough to do it justice. However much you see, one thing is for certain, you'll be back.

Facts + Figures

- **Population in 2003: 2,810,931.**
- **The official age of Rome in 2007 is 2,761 years.**
- **There have been 169 popes and 73 emperors.**
- **The area of the city covers 1,494sq km (577sq miles).**

SECRET KEYHOLE

Rome's most charming view is from Piazza dei Cavalieri di Malta on Aventine Hill. To find it, go to the left of the church of Santa Sabina and to the end of the piazza; look through the keyhole of the door (No. 3) of the Priory of the Knights of Malta. Through this tiny hole you will see a secret garden and an avenue of trees framing… but let's not spoil the surprise: see for yourself.

WATERY WASTE

More than 50 of Rome's fountains are fed by the waters of the Aqua Virgo, a source that the Romans first brought into the city in 19BC. It flows from the country-side outside the city, and feeds the Barcaccia fountain at the foot of the Spanish Steps, before supplying many others, including the most famous of them all, the Fontana di Trevi.

SWISS GUARD

The pope's official bodyguards are recruited from Switzerland's four pre-dominantly Catholic cantons. Each must be between 19 and 25, at least 1.75cm (5ft 8in) tall and remain unmarried dur-ing their tour of duty. Their distinctive uniforms were designed by Michelangelo in the hues of the Medici popes—red, yellow and blue.

A Short Stay in Rome

DAY 1

Morning Take breakfast in a café in **Campo de' Fiori** (▷ 48), a pretty square whose market makes a lively start to the day. Then glance at Piazza Farnese before walking east through the quiet streets of the Ghetto to Piazza Venezia and up the ramp to **Piazza del Campidoglio** (▷ 34).

Mid-morning Look around the piazza, dipping into the church of **Santa Maria in Aracoeli** (▷ 35) and the **Musei Capitolini** (▷ 28–29). Or make straight for the **Foro Romano** (▷ 26–27), **Palatino Hill** (▷ 34) and the **Colosseum** (▷ 24–25)—take the alley and steps to the rear left of Piazza del Campidoglio for a wonderful view of the Forum.

Lunch There are several restaurants near the Colosseum, notably **Pasquilino** (▷ 38). Alternatively, buy a snack in **Cavour 313** (▷ 37) or the café at the Monumento a Vittorio Emanuele II—it has great views over the Foro Romano and **Fori Imperiali** (▷ 33).

Afternoon Visit the **Palazzo-Galleria Doria Pamphilj** (▷ 44–45) and see the **Colonna di Marco Aurelio** (▷ 51) before walking to the **Fontana di Trevi** (▷ 78). Then walk to **Piazza di Spagna** for the Spanish Steps (▷ 81). If you want to shop, now is the time to do so, for the streets on and around nearby Via Condotti contain Rome's best stores. If not, and you want more culture, take a short walk east to the **Palazzo Barberini** (▷ 80), passing **Santa Maria delle Concezione** (▷ 87) on the way.

Dinner Take a bus or taxi to Trastevere, which has a wide choice of places to eat (▷ 73–74).

Evening Trastevere is not the cutting-edge nightlife district it once was, but its streets remain some of Rome's prettiest places to wander after dark.

DAY 2

Morning Today explore central Rome and the **Vatican** (▷ 96–97). If you want to do the museums justice, and beat some of the crowds, you'll need at least a morning and may wish to start the day there—or save them for another, longer visit. Otherwise, have breakfast in **Piazza Navona** (▷ 49) Rome's grandest square (or in **Bar della Pace**, ▷ 58, just off it), before the crowds arrive. Then walk east to the **Pantheon** (▷ 46–47) via San Luigi dei Francesi, also seeing **Santa Maria sopra Minerva** (▷ 50).

Mid-morning Take a coffee in **La Tazza d'Oro** (▷ 60). Then walk down Via delle Coppelle to see **Sant'Agostino** (▷ 52) and the superb **Palazzo Altemps** (▷ 42–43). Walk back toward Piazza Navona and explore Via dei Coronari and/or Via del Governo Vecchio or Via dei Banchi Nuovi, three of central Rome's most interesting streets.

Lunch The streets around Piazza Navona have plenty of bars and restaurants for lunch or a snack.

Afternoon Depending on time, and whether you want to see the Vatican museums, visit the **Castel Sant'Angelo** (▷ 95). Then make for the museums, or, for a more leisurely time, confine yourself to **St. Peter's** (▷ 94).

Dinner The area around St. Peter's is not great for dining, so take the 64 bus back to the heart of the city. The streets around Piazza Navona and Campo de' Fiori have plenty of restaurants.

Evening Join the throng in Piazza Navona, indulging in a famous *tartufo* ice cream from **Tre Scalini** (▷ 60). Or have a drink in one of the area's many bars. For peace and quiet, walk east to the **Ghetto** (▷ 67), whose streets are often deserted, despite being minutes from the nighttime hubbub.

►►►

Basilica di San Pietro
▷ **94** The Roman Catholic Church's principal shrine and spiritual focus.

Castel Sant'Angelo
▷ **95** A museum that was formerly a mausoleum and a fortress.

Colosseo ▷ **24–25**
The largest surviving ancient Roman structure in the world.

Villa Giulia ▷ **85**
Splendidly housed in the Villa Giulia is the National Etruscan Museum.

Villa Farnesina ▷ **66**
Peace and tranquillity away from the city noise set in lovely surroundings.

Santa Maria sopra Minerva ▷ **50** A touch of Gothic amid Rome's prevailing Renaissance and baroque architecture.

Santa Maria Maggiore
▷ **32** Contains the city's highest bell tower and features a sumptuous interior.

Santa Maria in Trastevere ▷ **64–65** A rare medieval church on the right bank of the River Tiber.

Santa Maria del Popolo
▷ **84** A must for art lovers, with works from some of the great names.

San Clemente ▷ **31**
▲ Remains of a temple to the
▲ Persian god Mithras with
▲ splendid mosaics.

Museo dei Fori Imperiali Trajan's Market ▷ **30**
Fascinating museum where excavations continue.

Piazza Navona ▷ **49**
A superb baroque city space and the setting for three magnificent fountains.

Villa Giulia

Villa Strohl Fern

Santa Maria del Popolo

AROUND THE VATICAN
91–98

Musei Vaticani

CITTÀ DEL VATICANO

Cappella Sistina

Basilica di San Pietro

Castel Sant'Angelo

Palazzo Altemps

CENTRAL ROME
39–60

Piazza Navona

Pantheon

Santa Maria sopra Minerva

Piazza Campo de' Fiori

Monte di Gallo

Monte Gianicolo

Villa Farnesina

Santa Maria in Trastevere

TRASTEVERE AND THE SOUTH
61–74

TRASTEVERE

Ostia Antica

These pages are a quick guide to the Top 25, which are described in more detail later. Here they are listed alphabetically and the tinted background shows which area they are in.

Fontana di Trevi ▷ 78
Nicola Salvi's baroque masterpiece and Rome's most popular fountain.

Foro Romano ▷ 26–27
The heart of ancient Rome and one of the city's most evocative sites.

Museo e Galleria Borghese ▷ 79 Beloved museum with great art in beautiful surroundings.

Musei Capitolini ▷ 28–29 The oldest collection in the world, with more than 1,300 works.

Musei Vaticani & Cappella Sistina ▷ 96–97 Supreme treasures spanning more than 3,000 years.

Ostia Antica ▷ 102–103 Ancient ruins, pine trees and wild spring flowers make the perfect setting.

Palazzo Altemps ▷ 42–43 A superb Renaissance building with top-class Classical sculpture.

Palazzo Barberini ▷ 80 Beautiful palazzo named after the powerful Barberini family.

Palazzo-Galleria Doria Pamphilj ▷ 44–45 An important art collection displayed in a beautiful palace.

Palazzo Massimo alle Terme ▷ 82–83 Some of Rome's most magnificent Classical treasures.

NORTHERN ROME 75–90

Museo e Galleria Borghese

Villa Borghese

SALARIO

Incio

Galoppatoio

Piazza di Spagna

Palazzo Barberini

Fontana di Trevi

Palazzo Massimo alle Terme

Monte Quirinale

Palazzo-Galleria Doria Pamphilj

Monte Viminale

Santa Maria Maggiore

Museo dei Fori Imperiali e Mercati Traianei

Musei Capitolini

Monte Capitolino

Monte Esquilino

Foro Romano

Monte Palatino

Colosseo

San Clemente

AVENTINO

THE ANCIENT CITY 21–38

Monte Aventino

Celio

Villa Celimontana

Piazza di Spagna ▷ 81
Site of the city's most stunning stairway, the Spanish Steps.

Piazza Campo de 'Fiori ▷ 48 A picturesque and atmospheric square in the heart of the city.

Pantheon ▷ 46–47 The best-preserved building from the Roman world; the last resting place of Raphael.

◀ ◀ ◀

Shopping

Rome was once the market place of an empire that embraced much of the known world. These days it has a more humble place in the shopping firmament. This said, all the great Italian retail staples—food, wine, fashion, shoes, leatherware and clothing— are well represented, and the city is a good source of art, antiques, traditional crafts and artisan products such as furniture.

More for your Money

Mid-price shoes and clothes represent good value for the money; you will find them in countless shops around the new city, but particularly Via Nazionale, Via del Tritone and Via del Corso. The same streets are also dotted with small specialist shops selling good-quality bags, gloves and other leatherware. The sprawling market in an ex-barracks near Piazza Vittorio Emanuele II, where most Romans do their shopping, is also a good source of clothes and shoes, as well as pots, pans and kitchenware with an Italian stamp (such as coffee-makers). In stylish Rome, even inexpensive clothes tend to be good quality and well-cut.

Designer Names

At the other sartorial extreme, most of the great Italian and European fashion houses have shops in the city: Gucci, Prada, Armani are all here, mostly in the grid of streets around Via

Great fashion houses sit side by side on Via Condotti, with the occasional gelateria in between for refreshment

---

ANTIQUES

It is no wonder, given Rome's long history, that the city is a treasury of antiques. Prices are often high, but the range of objects—Etruscan, Roman, Renaissance, baroque and other items—is unrivalled. For paintings and prints, head for Via Margutta, which also has a scattering of galleries selling contemporary art and carpets, while for general antiques try Via Giulia, Via del Babuino (particularly for Persian carpets), Via dei Coronari, Via dell'Orso and Via del Monserrato. Also good, and with lower prices and less exclusive stock, are Via del Panico, Via del Pellegrino and Via dei Banchi Nuovi.

Condotti, an excellent source of high-class clothes, shoes, lingerie and accessories. Department stores have not really caught on, and only Coin and Rinascente are worth a visit.

Tempt your Taste Buds
Shopping for food has a unique charm in Rome, whether in the small area shops known as *alimentari*, or the specialist delicatessens in streets such as Via della Croce. The city's ancient markets, particularly Campo de' Fiori, are vibrant sources of provisions. Pasta in every shape and size, the finest extra virgin oil, *funghi porcini* (dried cep mushrooms), truffle oil and spices made good food buys.

Catholic Paraphernalia
The range of shops selling ecclesiastical items is vast. The largest concentration is around St. Peter's—look out for ceramic Swiss Guards and fluorescent rosaries. On Via dei Cestari all manner of ecclesiastic garb is available—if you ever daydreamed about buying a bishop's robe or a cardinal's hat, this is the place.

Fun for the Tourist
Rome has any number of shops and stalls selling plaster and plastic casts of famous statues. Around the tourist traps are plenty of souvenirs, from figures of gladiators to models of the Colosseum. Better-quality items, plus books, prints and artistic replicas, are sold in museum and gallery shops.

Something to take home—a culinary delight, a designer bag or an exclusive little number from a top name

---

MARBLED PAPER

Notebooks and other stationery items covered with marbled paper make wonderful souvenirs, which you can find in shops all over the city. The paper originated in Venice, where the technique arrived from the East in the 15th century, and is still handmade. The process involves floating multicolour pigments on liquid gum and combing the different colours, separated by ox-gall, into distinctive patterns. The paper is placed delicately on top, then lifted and hung up to dry.

Shopping by Theme

Whether you're looking for a department store, a quirky boutique, or something in between, you'll find it all in Rome. On this page shops are listed by theme. For a more detailed write-up, see the individual listings in Rome by Area.

ACCESSORIES AND LEATHER GOODS

Furla (▷ 89)
Gucci (▷ 89)
Mondello Ottica (▷ 56)
La Perla (▷ 89)

BOOKS AND STATIONERY

Almost Corner Bookshop (▷ 71)
Antica Libreria Croce (▷ 55)
Cartoleria Pantheon (▷ 55)
Feltrinelli (▷ 56)
Pineider (▷ 89)
Poggi (▷ 56)

DEPARTMENT STORES

Coin (▷ 37)
La Rinascente (▷ 89)

INTERIORS

Bassetti (▷ 55)
Casimon (▷ 71)
Culti (▷ 55)
Ginori (▷ 89)
House & Kitchen (▷ 56)
Lumières (▷ 71)
Maria Grazia Luffarelli (▷ 56)
Ornamentum (▷ 56)
Pandora (▷ 71)
Spazio Sette (▷ 56)

FOOD AND WINE

Al Monasteri (▷ 55)
Antica Enoteca (▷ 89)
Bottega del Cioccolata (▷ 37)
Castroni (▷ 98)
Drogheria Innocenzi (▷ 71)
Enoteca Al Goccetto (▷ 55)
Franchi (Benedetto Franchi, ▷ 98)
Panella (▷ 37)
Volpetti (▷ 71)

FOOTWEAR

AVC di Adriana Campanile (▷ 89)
Fausto Santini (▷ 89)
Ferragamo (▷ 89)

MEN'S FASHION

Battistoni (▷ 89)
Ermenegildo Zegna (▷ 89)

OUTDOOR MARKETS

Campo de' Fiori (▷ 55)
Mercato Andrea Doria (▷ 98)
Mercato di Via Sannio (▷ 37)
Piazza Coppelle (▷ 56)
Piazza San Cosimato (▷ 71)
Porta Portese (▷ 71)

WOMEN'S FASHION

Ethic (▷ 55)
Fabindia (▷ 55)
Giorgio Armani (▷ 89)
Marella (▷ 89)

Rome by Night

After dark the heat of a summer day gives way to balmy evenings and life takes to the streets, allowing you to share in the soft, sweet blandishments of *la dolce vita,* still as vibrant and seductive as in the heady 1950s. Bars and cafés fill with Romans at their sleek and well-dressed best, while Lotharios and lean-limbed starlets and wannabes glide around the city on snarling Vespas and in open-topped sports cars.

Roman Illuminations

The Pantheon and Colosseum are spectacular under floodlights and romantic under moonlight. St. Peter's takes on a different hue under Rome's velvety night skies—come at midnight or later and you may well have Piazza San Pietro to yourself. The experience is magical. Much the same can be said of Rome's other great set-pieces, Piazza Navona, the Trevi Fountain and Spanish Steps. Piazza Navona, like a great nocturnal salon, fills with street performers, food stalls, artists and locals and visitors there to see and be seen.

Under the Stars

If you prefer tranquillity then walk from one sleepy fountain-splashed piazza to the next, sip an aperitif in a flower-decked terrace or eat alfresco—one of Rome's pleasures. Alternatively, take in an open-air concert amid ancient Roman ruins or a beautiful Renaissance garden.

As night falls, and you move from café to bar, enjoy the city's illuminated sights along the way

---

NOCTURNAL STROLLS

Rome's trendiest after-dark areas are San Lorenzo, a student and working-class district east of the city, and working-class Testaccio, to the south. Both are some way from the heart of town. So if you don't need to be at the cutting edge, spend the night in Trastevere, an established area full of small squares and pretty streets. To escape its crowds, walk to the Pincio from the top of the Spanish Steps for great sunset views, or wander through the old Ghetto area south of Via delle Botteghe Oscure, beautifully deserted after dark.

Eating Out

In Rome prepare yourself for rich, sun-drenched tastes. Thousands of restaurants cater to every budget and provide every kind of dining experience. Eating is so much a social way of life that it is quite normal to spend several hours over a meal.

When to Eat

If you are eating breakfast in a bar, as many Romans do, you will find that most bars open at around 7–7.30am for cappuccino and a croissant. In hotels, breakfast usually starts at 8am, and includes cereal, cold meat and cheeses. Restaurants open for lunch at 12.30 or 1pm, and serve until about 3pm. Romans generally eat dinner late, so many restaurants don't open for evening meals until 8pm, although you will find some that open earlier. Many places, especially cafés and bars, stay open all day.

Where to Eat

There are several different types of eating establishments in Rome. A *ristorante* tends to be the most expensive, with pristine table linen and waiters. The *trattoria* is less formal, less expensive and often family-run. An *osteria* or *hostaria* can be basic, sometimes with paper tablecloths and no written menu, but can serve some of the best food. A *rosticceria* or *tavola calda* is a fast-food outlet serving mostly cold foods. If you want pizza, look for the sign *pizzeria forno a legno* to make sure that it is traditionally cooked in a wood-fired oven.

PRICE MATTERS

Although in theory restaurants are no longer allowed to add a bread and cover charge, many feign oblivion to this and just charge for the bread anyway. Normally service is not included, although a minority of establishments do still add it as a fixed item. In everyday pizzerias, a tip of 5 per cent is perfectly adequate, but in *ristoranti*, if the service has been good, 10 per cent would be acceptable. You should always be given a receipt after paying the bill as the restaurant could be fined if they don't issue one.

Pizza, pasta or something more substantial, whatever your choice, finish it off with an espresso coffee

Restaurants by Cuisine

There are restaurants to suit all tastes and budgets in Rome. On this page they are listed by cuisine. For a more detailed description of each restaurant, see Rome by Area.

BARS BY DAY

Antica Birreria Peroni (▷ 58)
Bar della Pace (▷ 58)
Freni e Friziono (▷ 74)
Gran Caffè Martini e Rossi (▷ 38)
Latteria del Gallo (▷ 59)
Salotto 42 (▷ 60)
San Clemente (▷ 38)
Vineria Reggio Giorgia (▷ 60)

COFFEE/PASTRIES

Antico Caffè Brasile (▷ 38)
Bibli (▷ 73)
Caffè Farnese (▷ 58)
Sant' Eustachio (▷ 60)
La Tazza d'Oro (▷ 60)
Volpetti Più (▷ 74)

FINE DINING

L'Altro Mastai (▷ 58)
Brunello Restaurant (▷ 90)
Checchino dal 1887 (▷ 73)
Il Convivio Troiani (▷ 58)
Le Jardin de Russie (▷ 90)
Il Pagliaccio (▷ 60)
La Pergola (▷ 98)

FISH/SEAFOOD

Alberto Ciarla (▷ 73)
Dur Filettaro a Santa Barbara (▷ 59)
La Rosetta (▷ 60)
San Teodoro (▷ 38)

GELATERIE

Alberto Pica (▷ 73)
Gelateria della Palma (▷ 59)
Il Gelato di San Crispino (▷ 90)
Giolitti (▷ 59)
Tre Scalini (▷ 60)

PIZZA/PASTA

Da Baffetto (▷ 58)
Dar Poeta (▷ 73)
Da Vittorio (▷ 74)
Est! Est! Est! (▷ 90)
Ivo (▷ 74)
Panattoni (▷ 74)

ROMAN/ITALIAN

Adriano (▷ 106)
Agate e Romeo (▷ 38)
Augusto (▷ 73)
Il Bacaro (▷ 58)
Borgo Nuovo (▷ 98)

Cacciani (▷ 106)
Checco Er Carettiere (▷ 73)
Ciccia Bomba (▷ 58)
Da Felice (▷ 73)
Da Francesco (▷ 59)
Dal Toscano (▷ 98)
Ditirambo (▷ 59)
Grappolo d'Oro (▷ 59)
Il Grottino della Sibilla dal 1826 (▷ 106)
'Gusto (▷ 59)
Paris (▷ 74)
Pasquilino (▷ 38)
Sora Lella (▷ 74)
Taverna Angelica (▷ 98)
Tucci (▷ 60)
Zarazà (▷ 106)

WORLD CUISINES

Charly's Saucière (▷ 38)
Giggetto (▷ 74)
Hasekura (▷ 38)
L'Eau Vive (▷ 59)
Piperno (▷ 74)
Thien Kim (▷ 60)

If You Like...

However you'd like to spend your time in Rome, these top
suggestions should help you tailor your ideal visit. Each sight or
listing has a fuller write-up elsewhere in the book.

BURNING THE MIDNIGHT OIL

Sit up late with the beautiful people in Bar della
Pace (▷ 58).
Share a glass or two of wine with the charac-
ters in the bars around Campo de' Fiori (▷ 48).
Visit one or more of the many clubs in the
Testaccio (▷ 72) nightlife district.

THE LAP OF LUXURY

Go mad in the chic designer stores in the streets
around Via dei Condotti (▷ 89).
Stay in one of the city's opulent five-star hotels,
notably the Hassler–Villa Medici (▷ 112).
Eat at Il Convivio Troiani or La Rosetta (▷ 58,
60), two of the city's best restaurants.

*Cafés in Campo dei Fiori
buzz at night (top). Spoil
yourself and stay in one
of Rome's top hotels
(above)*

TO KEEP YOUR CHILDREN HAPPY

Take them to the Bioparco in the Villa
Borghese (▷ 87).
Buy lots of ice cream, especially from
Giolitti or Gelateria della Palma (▷ 59).
Introduce them to the characters
dressed as centurions and gladiators out-
side the Colosseum (▷ 24–25).

SAVING FOR A RAINY DAY

Buy an integrated travel pass
(▷ 118–119) and save on public transport.
Visit Rome's art-crammed churches—
such as Santa Maria sopra Minerva
(▷ 50)—they are virtually all free.
Time your visit for the last Sunday of
the month, when the normally expensive Vatican museums (▷ 96–97) are free.

Posing outside the Colosseum (above right). Visit Santa Prassede for free (right)

A night of jazz (below). A hotel offering unparalleled views of the city (below middle)

AN EVENING OF ENTERTAINMENT

See what's playing at the Teatro dell'Opera di Roma (▷ 90).

Enjoy a night of blues or jazz at Big Mama (▷ 72).

Look out for posters advertising church recitals and other classical music concerts. In summer, many are held outdoors (▷ 37).

A MEMORABLE PLACE TO STAY

De Russie (▷ 112) broke the mold for luxury Rome hotels with its sleek and clean-lined contemporary design.

Join the rich and famous and stay at the Hassler-Villa Medici, with view of the Spanish Steps (▷ 112).

The pretty, ivy-covered Raphaël (▷ 112) is a tranquil, perfectly situated gem.

ROMANTIC SUPPERS

Dine outdoors in summer; try Panattoni (▷ 74), but almost any restaurant or pizzeria will do.

Splash out on a meal at L'Astro Mastai (▷ 58), for that special, intimate dining experience.

Buy a picnic and take it to the Pincio gardens (▷ 87) to watch the sunset over St. Peter's.

Eat Italian at a traditional trattoria (above) and shop in style on Via Condotti (below)

SPECIALTY SHOPPING

Via dei Coronari (▷ 55–56) and the streets nearby are the places for antiques and sumptuous fabrics.

Stroll down Via Margutta to take in its various art galleries (▷ 10, panel 55).

For designer clothes and accessories, it has to be Via Condotti (▷ 89).

A BREATH OF FRESH AIR

Get away from it all— Villa Borghese and Colle Oppio (below)

The Villa Borghese (▷ 87) park offers numerous walks and shady nooks.
Escape the crowds around the Forum by climbing the Palatino Hill (▷ 34).
If you don't have time to see the Gianicolo and Villa Doria Pamphilj above Trastevere, how about the closer Orto Botanico (▷ 68).

A TASTE OF TRADITION

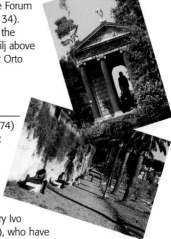

Long-established Giggetto (▷ 74) and Piperno (▷ 74) serve classic Roman-Jewish cuisine.
As its name suggests, Checchino dal 1887 (▷ 73) has been serving traditional Roman food for more than 120 years.
To sample pizza at its best, try Ivo (▷ 74) and Da Baffetto (▷ 58), who have served pizza to generations of Romans.

A GREAT CUP OF COFFEE

La Tazza d'Oro (▷ 60), a stone's throw from the Pantheon, is a temple to the espresso.
Sant' Eustachio (▷ 60) serves what many locals consider to be Rome's best cup of coffee.
Antico Caffè Brasile (▷ 38) knows its beans— Pope John Paul II once bought his coffee here.

THE WORLD'S BEST CLASSICAL SCULPTURE

After visiting the Musei Capitolini (below) move on to La Tazza d'Oro (above) for a great coffee

Visit the Palazzo Altemps (▷ 42–43) and Palazzo Massimo alle Terme (▷ 82–83), which have manageable and beautifully presented collections.
To see individual sculptural works go to the Museo Capitolini (▷ 28–29), with some of the city's most significant pieces.
The Laocoön (▷ 96) is the most celebrated of the Vatican museums' immense collection of sculptures.

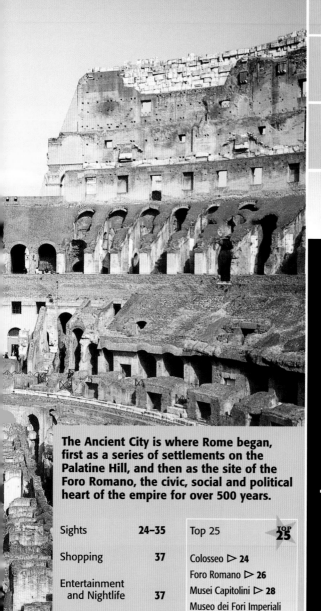

The Ancient City

The Ancient City is where Rome began, first as a series of settlements on the Palatine Hill, and then as the site of the Foro Romano, the civic, social and political heart of the empire for over 500 years.

Colosseo

HIGHLIGHTS

● Circumference walls
● Arches: 80 lower arches for the easy admission of crowds
● Doric columns: lowest arcade
● Ionic columns: central arcade
● Corinthian columns: upper arcade
● Underground cells
● Sockets that once housed binding metal clamps
● Vomitoria: interior exits and entrances
● Views from the upper levels

TIP

● The Colosseum's ticket office can be very busy—buy your ticket at the Palatine to avoid waiting, or online.

The Pantheon may be better preserved and the Forum more historically important, but no monument in Rome rivals the majesty of the Colosseum, the largest surviving structure from Roman antiquity.

Awe-inspring The Colosseum was begun by Emperor Vespasian in AD72 and inaugurated by his son, Titus, in AD80 with a gala that saw 5,000 animals slaughtered in a day (and 100 days of continuous games thereafter). Finishing touches to the 55,000-seat stadium were added by Domitian (AD81–96). Three types of columns support the arcades, and the walls are made of brick and volcanic tufa faced with marble blocks, which were once bound together by metal clamps. Its long decline began in the Middle Ages, with the pillaging of stone to build churches and palaces. The

Clockwise from far left: inside the Colosseum the various tiers are still very evident; the magnificent Colosseum is a daunting sight from all perspectives: close up, from a distance, illuminated at night or under an Italian sunset

desecration ended in 1744, when the structure was consecrated in memory of the Christians supposedly martyred in the arena (later research suggests they weren't). Clearing of the site and excavations began late in the 19th century.

Games Armed combat at the Colosseum went on for some 500 years. Criminals, slaves and gladiators fought each other or wild animals, often to the death. Women and dwarfs also wrestled, and mock sea battles were waged (the arena could be flooded via underground pipes). Spectators exercised the power of life and death over defeated combatants, by waving handkerchiefs to show mercy or by displaying a down-turned thumb to demand the finishing stroke. Survivors' throats were often cut anyway, and the dead were poked with a red-hot iron to make sure they had expired.

THE BASICS

✚ J7

✉ Piazza del Colosseo, Via dei Fori Imperiali

☎ 06 3996 7700; online booking www.pierreci.it

🕐 May–end Sep daily 9–7.30; Apr and Oct 9–6.30; Nov–end Mar 9–4.30. Last admission 1 hour before closing

Ⓜ Colosseo

🚌 3, 60, 75, 85, 87, 117, 175 to Piazza del Colosseo

♿ Poor to the interior; limited access from Via Celio Vibenna entrance

💰 Expensive (joint ticket with Palatino)

HIGHLIGHTS

● Temple of Antoninus and Faustina (AD141)
● Colonna di Foca (AD608)
● Arch of Septimius Severus (AD203)
● Curia (Senate House, 80BC)
● Portico of the Dei Consentes (AD367)
● Temple of Saturn (AD284)
● Santa Maria Antiqua, the Forum's oldest church, dating back to the 5th century AD
● Arch of Titus

TIPS

● Making sense of the Forum is quite a challenge—use an audioguide to get more out of your visit.
● Take something to drink as there are no bars in the Forum area.

The Roman Forum was the political and civic heart of the empire—the biggest and most important of the forums in the world. One of the most evocative of all ruins, it is where Mark Antony delivered his 'Friends, Romans, Countrymen' speech after Julius Cæsar's assassination.

History The Forum (Foro Romano) started life as a marsh between the Palatine and Capitoline hills, taking its name from a word meaning 'outside the walls'. Later, unfortunately, it became a rubbish dump, and then, having been drained, a market-place and a religious shrine. In time it acquired all the structures of Rome's burgeoning civic, social and political life. Over the many centuries consuls, emperors and senators have embellished it with magnificent temples, courts and basilicas.

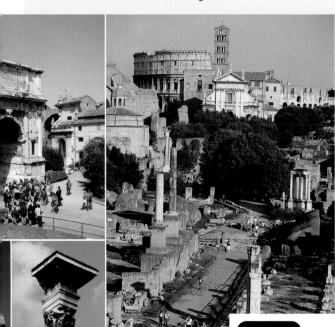

Clockwise from far left: lone columns and fallen masonary give few clues to the Forum's former impressiveness; Marble Arch of Titus; detail of relief decoration and frieze on the remains of the Forum market; a remaining Corinthian column; the view across the Forum, with the Colosseum in the background

Forum Two millennia of plunder and decay have left a mishmash of odd pillars and jumbled stones, which nonetheless can begin to make vivid sense given a plan and some imagination. The Rostrum, well known as being the setting for Mark Antony's famous speach, was the platform of a great many historic moments.

Beauty Spots Today orange trees, oleanders and cypresses line the paths, and grasses and wild-flowers flourish among the ancient remains. Somewhat aloof from the rubble stands the ele-gantly restored House of the Vestal Virgins (Casa della Vestali), home of a sect formed of daughters of the Roman nobility chosen to serve Vesta, goddess of hearth and home. There were always six in number who served 30 years from age six to 36.

THE BASICS

✚ H7

✉ Entrances alongside Arco di Settimio Sevoro, near Arco di Tito and Largo Romolo e Remo on Via dei Fori Imperiali

☎ 06 699 0110 or 06 3996 7700

◷ Daily 9 to 1 hour before dusk

Ⓜ Colosseo

🚌 60, 75, 84, 85, 87, 117, 271, 571, 810, 850 to Via dei Fori Imperiali

♿ Access difficult to much of site

💷 Forum free. Palatine expensive (joint ticket with Colosseum)

HIGHLIGHTS

Palazzo Nuovo
● Replica equestrian piazza statue of Marcus Aurelius
● *Capitoline Venus*: the life-size statue of the goddess
● The colossal statue of Marforio above the fountain in the courtyard

Palazzo dei Conservatori
● Caravaggio's painting of St. John the Baptist
● Bronze of Lupa Capitolina
● The original, restored statue of Marcus Aureilius
● Giant head and fragments of Constantine's statue

TIP

● Allow plenty of time and be prepared to concentrate. This is not the easiest museum and not for the fainthearted.

Few in number, but outstanding, the Greek and Roman sculptures in the Capitoline Museums (Palazzo Nuovo and Palazzo dei Conservatori) make a far more accessible introduction to the subject than the Vatican Museums.

Palazzo Nuovo The Capitoline Museums occupy two palaces on opposite sides of the Piazza del Campidoglio and are linked by an underground passage. Both have recently been restored. Designed by Michelangelo, the Palazzo Nuovo (on the north side) contains most of the finest pieces. Few more impressive than the magnificent equestrian statue of the emperor and philosopher Marcus Aurelius, which is, surprisingly, a well-made replica of the 2nd-century AD original moved into the museum next door for restoration after damage in

Clockwise from far left: Spinario, an endearing bronze statue; the remains of Constantine's giant statue; a satyr, part of the ancient statuary collection; the Dying Gaul, *a wonderful example of Classical sculpture; the serene* Capitoline Venus *stands in splendid isolation; one of two statues representing the Nile and the Tiber*

1981. Among the sculptures inside are celebrated Roman copies in marble of Greek originals, including the *Dying Gaul*, *Wounded Amazon*, *Capitoline Venus* and the discus thrower *Discobolus*. In the Sala degli Imperatori is a portrait gallery of busts of Roman emperors.

Palazzo dei Conservatori As well as the Pinacoteca Capitolina art gallery and original Marcus Aurelies statue, the Conservatori is distinguished by a courtyard featuring the head and fragments of the 4th-century AD statue of Constantine, originally 12m (40ft) high. Also inside is the 5th-century BC Etruscan *Lupa Capitolina*, the famous she-wolf suckling Romulus and Remus (the twins were added by Antonio Pollaiuolo in 1510). Paintings include works by Caravaggio, Velázquez, Titian, Veronese and Van Dyck.

THE BASICS

www.museicapitolini.org
✚ G6
✉ Musei Capitolini, Piazza del Campidoglio 1
☎ 06 6710 2475 or 06 3996 7800
🕐 Tue–Sun 9–8
🚌 40, 44, 64 and all other services to Piazza Venezia
♿ Poor: steps to Piazza del Campidoglio
💰 Expensive; combined Capitolini Card available

Museo dei Fori Imperiali and Trajan's Market

Trajan's Market climbs Quirinal Hill (right) to the Torre delle Milizie (right)

HIGHLIGHTS

● The view of the 13th-century Torre delle Milizie
● The intricate spiral bas-relief that climbs Trajan's Column, depicting victories in battle
● Basilica Ulpia, which became the most important in the life of the Empire, dedicated not to religion but justice

Like the burgeoning Roman Empire itself, the city's uncovered remains continue to grow, even into the 3rd millennium when this grand museum and surrounding areas ruins fully emerged.

Trajan's Market Mercati Traianei were originally thought to have been the precursor of modern shopping malls—a group of commercial buildings constructed in the 2nd century AD as a semicircular range of halls on three levels. Two of the levels survive in excellent condition. But it's now thought the 'markets' were more probably a new hub for politics and justice inaugurated by the Emperor Trajan in 112AD before his death in 117AD, and the 150 or so booths and halls of the structure were offices once populated by civil servants, though some at ground level may have been shops. Either way, they present a magnificent spectacle.

Museum The labyrinthine museum within the Trajan's Market is an absorbing peep into Rome's distant past. Opened in 2007, it presents the grand Imperial Fora using modern techniques including film and pictographic illustration, as well as items unearthed in recent excavations in the area. The external viewing gallery gives a splendid view, not only of the surrounding ruins, but the whole Fora area of ancient Rome, as well as the 113AD Trajan's Column, which stands at 30m (100ft), built of hollow marble. Additionally, since 2008, the Museo dei Fori Imperiali has also started functioning as a venue for contemporary arts with regular displays of painting and also specially convened exhibitions.

Two of San Clemente's treasures: 12th-century mosaics (left) and the Mithraic temple (right)

San Clemente

No site in Rome reveals as vividly the layers of history that underpin the city as this beautiful medieval ensemble built over a superbly preserved 4th-century church and the remains of a 3rd-century Mithraic temple.

The upper church The present San Clemente, which was named after Rome's fourth pope, was built between 1108 and 1184 to replace an earlier one that was sacked by the Normans in 1084. Almost untouched since, its medieval interior is dominated by the 12th-century marble panels of the choir screen and pulpits and the glittering 12th-century apse mosaic, *The Triumph of the Cross*. Equally captivating are the *Life of St. Catherine* frescos (1428–31) by Masolino da Panicale.

Below ground Steps descend to the lower church, which retains traces of 8th- to 11th-century frescos of San Clemente and the legends of Sts. Alessio and Sisinnio. More steps lead deeper into the twilight world of the best-preserved of the 12 Mithraic temples uncovered in Rome. (Mithraism was a popular, men-only cult, eclipsed by Christianity.) Here are an altar with a bas-relief of Mithras ritually slaying a bull, and the triclinium, used for banquets and rites. Excavations are revealing parts of the temple, and the 1,900-year-old remains of buildings, streets and an underground stream, which you can hear even today, that may have formed part of ancient Rome's drainage system.

THE BASICS

🔲 K7
✉ Via di San Giovanni in Laterano
☎ 06 7045 1018
🕐 Mon–Sat 9–12.30, 3–6, Sun 10–12.30, 3–6
🚌 60, 85, 87, 117, 175 to Piazza del Colosseo or 85, 117, 850 to Via di San Giovanni in Laterano
♿ Church free; excavations moderate

HIGHLIGHTS

● Choir screen
● Chapel of St. Catherine: fresco cycle
● Ciborio: altar canopy
● Apse mosaic: *The Triumph of the Cross*
● Monument to Cardinal Roverella, Giovanni Dalmata (upper church)
● Fresco: *Miracle of San Clemente*
● Fresco: *Legend of Sisinnio*
● Triclinium
● Altar of Mithras: bas-relief of Mithras slaying the bull

Santa Maria Maggiore

TOP 25

Ferdinando Fuga's 18th-century façade (right) conceals a beautiful interior (left)

THE BASICS

➕ K5

✉ Piazza di Santa Maria Maggiore and Piazza dell'Esquilino

☎ 06 483 195 or 06 581 4802

🕐 Apr–end Sep daily 7–7/8; Oct–end Mar 7–6.30/7. Loggia: guided tours Mar–end Oct daily 9–6.30; Nov–end Feb 9–1

🚇 Termini or Cavour

🚌 C3, 16, 70, 71, 75, 84, 360 to Piazza di Santa Maria Maggiore

♿ Poor: access is easiest from Piazza di Santa Maria Maggiore

🎫 Church free; Loggia inexpensive

HIGHLIGHTS

● The world's oldest icon of the Virgin Mary, said to be 1,000 years old, in the Pauline Chapel

● Bernini's painting of St. Cajetan Holding The Holy Child

● The Crypt of the Nativity with tombs of many orimi-nent men of the church

Santa Maria Maggiore is, justifiably so, considered Rome's finest Early Christian basilica, which is largely thanks to its magnificent mosaic-swathed interior.

History According to a myth, the Virgin appeared to Pope Liberius on 5 August AD352, and told him to build a church exactly where snow would fall the next day. Although it was summer, snow fell, marking the outlines of a basilica on the Esquiline Hill. Legend aside, the church probably dates from AD430, though the campanile (the tallest in Rome at 75m/246ft) was added in 1377 and the interior and exterior were altered in the 13th and 18th centuries. The coffered ceiling, attributed to Giuliano da Sangallo, was reputedly gilded with the first gold to arrive from the New World, a gift from Spain to Alexander VI (note his Borgia bull emblems).

Rich decoration Beyond the general grandeur, the main treasures are the 36 mosaics in the architraves of the nave, 5th-century depictions of the lives of Moses, Abraham, Isaac and Jacob, framed by some 40 ancient columns. Also compelling are the mosaics in the loggia and on the triumphal arch. In the 13th-century apse are mosaics by Jacopo Torriti, the pinnacle of Rome's medieval mosaic tradition. Other highlights include the Cappella Sistina (tomb of Pope Sixtus V) by Domenico Fontana, 1588; the Cappella Paolina, built by Paul V (1611); and Giovanni di Cosma's tomb of Cardinal Rodriguez (1299). The high altar reputedly contains a relic of Christ's crib.

More to See

ARCO DI COSTANTINO

Triumphal arches, like celebratory columns, were usually raised as monuments to military achievement, in this case the victory of Emperor Constantine over his imperial rival Maxentius. It was one of the last great monuments to be built in ancient Rome, and at 21m (69ft) high and 26m (85ft) wide it is also the largest and best-preserved of the city's arches. Most of its reliefs were taken from earlier buildings, partly out of pragmatism and partly out of a desire to link Constantine's glories with those of the past. The battle scenes of the central arch show Trajan at war with the Dacians, while another describes a boar hunt and sacrifice to Apollo.

⊞ J7 ⊠ Piazza del Colosseo-Via di San Gregorio, Via dei Fori Imperiali ⏰ Always open ⓜ Colosseo 🚌 60, 75, 85, 87, 117, 175, C3 to Piazza del Colosseo 💵 Free

CIRCO MASSIMO

This enormous grassy arena follows the outline of a stadium once capable of seating 300,000 people. Created to satisfy the passionate Roman appetite for chariot racing, and the prototype for almost all subsequent racecourses, it was begun around 326BC and modified frequently before the occasion of its last recorded use under Totila the Ostrogoth in AD549. Much of the original structure was robbed of its stone—old monuments were often ransacked for building materials—but the *spina* (the circuit's dividing wall) remains, marked by a row of cypresses, the ruins of the imperial box and the open arena, now a public park. Avoid after dark.

⊞ H8 ⊠ Via del Circo Massimo ⏰ Always open ⓜ Circo Massimo 🚌 60, 75, 81, 175, 628, 673, C3 to Piazza di Porta Capena 💵 Free

FORI IMPERIALI

Including the Foro Romano (▷ 26), all five of the Imperial Forums that are featured in the Museo dei Fori Imperiali (▷ 30) stretch out between the museum area and the Colosseum, and it's worth the walk to see them all. Built as political and commercial hubs by successive emperors, they have been

Cast in evening light, the Arch of Constantine

The remains of the Tempio di Saturno, Fori Imperiali

ruthlessly plundered over the centuries, and may seem like a haphazard collection of columns and tumbled stone, but seeing them close-up can be quite momentous. Excavations are ongoing and what has been unearthed represents only half of the original forums.

➕ H6 ✉ Via dei Fori Imperiali ☎ 06 679 7786; Visitor Centre 06 679 7702 🕐 Guided tour only, check with Visitor Centre for times 🚇 Colosseo 🚌 75, 84, 87, 117, 175 to Via dei Fori Imperiali 💶 Moderate

PALATINO HILL

After a stroll around the Forum it's worth making time to climb the Palatine Hill to enjoy this peaceful spot. Orange groves, cypresses and endless drowsy corners, all speckled with flowers and ancient stones, make up the Farnesian Garden (Orti Farnesiani), which were laid out in the 16th century over the ruins of the palace that once stood here.

➕ H7 ✉ Entrances from Via di San Gregorio 30 and other entrances to Roman Forum ☎ 06 3996 7700 🕐 Daily 9–1 hour before dusk 🚇 Colosseo 🚌 75, 84, 87, 117, 175 to Via dei Fori Imperiali 💶 Expensive (joint ticket with Colosseum)

PIAZZA DEL CAMPIDOGLIO

This piazza was designed by Michelangelo for Emperor Charles V's triumphal entry into Rome in 1536 on the Capitoline, the most famous of Rome's seven hills and the hub of the Roman Empire. The magnificent buildings that stand on three sides of the square—the Palazzo Senatorio, the Palazzo Nuovo and the Palazzo dei Conservatori, were part of his scheme.

➕ G6 ✉ Piazza del Campidoglio 🚇 Colosseo 🚌 All services to Piazza Venezia

SAN GIOVANNI IN LATERANO

Until the 14th century when the Popes moved to the Vatican, San Giovanni was the pontiff's seat and the focus of Christianity. It's no accident that it was modelled on St. Peters when the 4th-century original was rebuilt in the 17th century after Barbarians, earthquakes and fires destroyed it. Inside and out it is a treasury of tradition and legend.

The vast inside of San Giovanni in Laterano

Remains laid out beneath the ruins on Palatine Hill

⊞ L8 ⊠ Piazza San Giovanni in Laterano
☎ 06 6988 6433 ⏰ Church Apr–end Sep
daily 7–7 (Oct–end Mar until 6/6.30). Cloisters
daily 9–12, 4–6 (5 in winter) 🚇 San
Giovanni 🚌 3, 16, 81, 85 87, 117, 850 to
Piazza Via di San Giovanni 👋 Inexpensive

SAN PIETRO IN VINCOLI

San Pietro in Vincoli is a thoroughly appealing church with an admired Michelangelo statue of Moses, one of the most powerful of all the artist's monumental sculptures. San Pietro in Vincoli takes its name from the chains (*vincoli*) proudly kept in the coffer with bronze doors under the high altar. It is said they are the chains used to bind St. Peter while he was held captive in the Mamertine prison.

⊞ J6 ⊠ Piazza di San Pietro in Vincoli 4a
☎ 06 488 2865 ⏰ Daily 8–12/12.30,
3/3.30–6/7 🚇 Colosseo or Cavour 🚌 75,
84 to Via Cavour or 60, 75, 85, 87, 117, 175 to
Piazza del Colosseo 🦽 Good 👋 Free

SANTA MARIA IN ARACOELI

Perched atop the Capitoline Hill, Santa Maria in Aracoeli, with its glorious ceiling, fine frescos and soft chandelier-lit interior, is a calm retreat from the ferocious traffic of Piazza Venezia. The flight of 124 steep steps approaching Santa Maria was built in 1348 to celebrate either the end of a plague epidemic or the Holy Year proclaimed for 1350. The church is first recorded in AD574, but even then it was old. Most of the present structure dates from 1260.

⊞ G6 ⊠ Piazza d'Aracoeli ☎ 06 679 8155
⏰ Daily 7–12, 4–6 or dusk 🚌 40, 44, 46,
62, 64, 70, 80 and all other services to Piazza
Venezia 🦽 Poor: steep steps to main
entrance or steps to Piazza del Campidoglio
👋 Free

VILLA CELIMONTANA

Set on one of the southern hills of ancient Rome and scattered with the remains of ancient buildings, this is one of Rome's lesser-known parks, easily accessible from the Colosseum and San Giovanni in Laterano.

⊞ J8 ⊠ Piazza della Navicella ⏰ Daily
7–dusk 🚌 3 to Via dei Parco del Celio or
117, 673 to Via Claudia 👋 Free

A statue of Marcus Aurelius takes the stage in Piazza del Campidoglio

Michelangelo's monumental statue of Moses, in the church of San Pietro in Vincoli

Shopping

BOTTEGA DEL CIOCCOLATO

A blissful Italian chocolate shop. Most goodies are produced from a 19th-century Piedmont recipe; others are 'secrets of old masters'. There are period cupboards and shelves, and a mirror reflects the chocolate creations along the wall in jars.

⊞ J6 ✉ Via Leonina 82 ☎ 06 482 1473 ◷ Mon–Sat 9.30–7.30; closed Sep

COIN

www.coin.it

One of Rome's most popular department stores is a modern, mainly glass building with cosmetics, home furnishings, kitchenware, toys and fashions. The top floor is dedicated to home exhibitions. Prices are higher than in the average store.

⊞ M8 ✉ Piazza Appio 7 ☎ 06 708 0020 ◷ Daily 10–8.30 (Sun 10.30–8.30)

MERCATO DI VIA SANNIO

This market in the shadow of San Giovanni in Laterano sells bags, belts, shoes, toys and inexpensive clothes. Other stands nearby peddle more interesting bric-a-brac.

⊞ M8 ✉ Via Sannio ◷ Mon–Fri 10–1.30, Sat 10–6

PANELLA

For more than a century, Panella has sold dozens of varieties of bread and cakes, and it has the largest selection of homemade *grissini* (bread stick) in Rome. The back rooms are packed with hard-to-find ingredients.

⊞ K6 ✉ Via Merulana 54–55 ☎ 06 487 2344 ◷ Mon–Sat 8–2, 5–8, Sun 8–2

Entertainment and Nightlife

CAVOUR 313

At the Forum end of Via Cavour, this easily missed wine bar has a relaxed, student feel. Good snacks from the bar and wine by the glass or bottle.

⊞ H6 ✉ Via Cavour 313 ☎ 06 678 5496 ◷ Mon–Sat 12.30–2.30, 7.30–12.30 (also Sun 7.30–12.30 Oct–end May) 🚍 75, 84, 117 to Via Cavour or 84, 85, 87, 175 to Via dei Fori Imperiali

DRUID'S DEN

Friendly and realistic Irish pub that appeals to Romans and expats alike. Also try the Fiddler's Elbow, a popular sister pub around the corner at Via dell'Olmata 43.

⊞ K6 ✉ Via San Martino ai Monti 28 ☎ 06 4890 4781

MUSIC OUTDOORS

Alfresco recitals often take place throughout the city in summer. Locations include the cloisters of Santa Maria della Pace; the Villa Doria Pamphilj; in the grounds of the Villa Giulia; and in the Area Archeologica del Teatro di Marcello from July to September (as part of the Estate al Tempietto, also known as the Concerti del Tempietto). Note that the venues may change from year to year.

◷ Daily 5pm–2am 🚇 Cavour 🚍 75, 84, 117 to Via Cavour or 16, 70, 71, 360 to Piazza Santa Maria Maggiore

TEATRO COLOSSEO

www.teatrocolosseo.it

In the shadow of the mighty Colosseum, this venue is a rarity for Rome—a theatre that sometimes stages English-language plays. It showcases young directors and actors, and the small stage suits one-person shows.

⊞ J7 ✉ Via Capo d'Africa 5 ☎ 06 700 4932 ◷ Sep–end Jun Mon–Sat 10–1, 3–7 🚇 Colosseo 🚍 30

Restaurants

PRICES

Prices are approximate, based on a 3-course meal for one person.

€€€   over €50
€€   €30–€50
€   under €30

AGATA E ROMEO (€€€)

www.agataeromeo.it

It is worth putting up with a less-than-perfect position south of Termini because this homey, one Michelin star, family-run restaurant serves some of the city's best and most imaginative modern Roman cooking.

➕ K6 ✉ Via Carlo Alberto 45 ☎ 06 446 6115
🕐 Mon–Fri 12.30–2.30, 7.30–10; closed 1–27 Jan, 6–28 Aug 🚌 70, 71, 360 to Via Carlo Alberto

ANTICO CAFFÈ BRASILE (€)

A superb variety of beans and ground coffee is sold from huge sacks or at the bar. Try the 'Pope's blend': John Paul II bought his coffee here before his pontificate.

➕ J6 ✉ Via dei Serpenti 23 ☎ 06 488 2319 🕐 Mon–Sat 6am–8pm, Sun 7–8; closed Sun Jun–end Aug 🚌 60, 63, 64, 70, 117, 170 to Via Nazionale or 75, 84, 117 to Via Cavour

CHARLY'S SAUCIÈRE (€€)

Homey and established, offering reliable French and Swiss staples.

➕ L8 ✉ Via di San Giovanni in Laterano 268–270
☎ 06 7049 5666 🕐 Tue–Fri 12.30–2.30, Mon–Sat 7.30–10.30; closed 2 weeks in Aug 🚌 85, 117, 850 to Via San Giovanni in Laterano

GRAN CAFFÈ MARTINI E ROSSI (€)

Bar/restaurant popular with locals, and what better location could it have than looking across to the Palatine Hill, with the Colosseo across the road? Good-value all-inclusive menus, plus snacks and vegetarian dishes.

➕ J7 ✉ Piazza del Colosseo ☎ 06 700 4431 🕐 Daily 9am–1am 🚌 85, 87, 117

HASEKURA (€–€€)

Rome's best Japanese food; good set-price

ROMAN SPECIALTIES

Roman preferences—though they are by no means confined to the city—include pastas like *bucatini all'amatriciana* (tomato sauce, salt pork and chilli peppers); *spaghetti alla carbonara* (egg, bacon, pepper and cheese); and *gnocchi alla Romana* (small potato or semolina dumplings with tomato or butter). The best-known main course is *saltimbocca alla Romana* (veal scallops with ham and sage, cooked in wine and butter). Also traditional are *trippa* (tripe), *cervelli* (brains) and *coda alla vaccinara* (oxtail).

menus, with the Forum and Colosseum close by. Popular with actors and celebrities.

➕ J6 ✉ Via dei Serpenti 27 ☎ 06 483 648 🕐 Mon–Sat 12–2.30, 7–10.30; closed Aug 🚇 Cavour 🚌 71, 84 to Via Cavour

PASQUILINO (€€)

A simple, long-established *trattoria* with good, robust food a few minutes east of the Colosseum.

➕ K7 ✉ Via S.S Quattro Coronati 66 ☎ 06 700 4576 🕐 Tue–Sun 12.30–2.30, 7.30–11; closed 2 weeks in Aug 🚇 Colosseo 🚌 85 to Via di San Giovanni in Laterano

SAN CLEMENTE (€)

This bar/pizzeria is a great place to refuel between the Colosseo and the basilica of San Giovanni in Laterano. Three vaulted rooms and a terrace offer decent inexpensive food.

➕ K7 ✉ Via di San Giovanni Laterano 124 ☎ 06 7045 0944 🕐 Daily 7am–1am 🚇 Colosseo or San Giovanni 🚌 85, 87, 117 to Via di San Giovanni in Laterano

SAN TEODORO (€€€)

Set among the medieval houses in the shadow of the Forum, this established restaurant specializes in fish and seafood. Dine alfresco on traditional delights and lighter dishes. Reserve ahead.

➕ H7 ✉ Via dei Fienili, 49 ☎ 066 78 09 33 🕐 Daily 1–3.15, 8–11.30; closed Sun Nov–end Mar 🚇 Colosseo

Here, most of the great churches, palaces and squares of the city's medieval, baroque and Renaissance heyday sit beside museums, monuments and cobbled streets filled with cafés, shops and restaurants.

Colonna di
Marco Aurelio

Piazza
Montecitorio

Piazza
Colonna

Museo Nazionale
delle Paste
Alimentari

Via delle Muratte

Via della Dataria

Via degli Umiltà

Monte Quirinale

VIA DEL QUIRINALE

Piazza del
Quirinale

Via Piacenza

Via Parma

Via della Consulta

Castini

iel Seminario

Sant'Ignazio
di Loyola

Santa Maria
sopra Minerva

Lucchesi

Santi
Apostoli

Villa
Colonna

VIA XXIV MAGGIO

Palazzo-Galleria
Doria Pamphilj

Piazza
dei Santi
Apostoli

EMANUELE II   VIA DEL PLEBISCITO

San Marco

Museo del
Palazzo
Venezia

Piazza
Venezia

Chiesa
del Gesù

Botteghe   Oscure

Crypta
Balbi

Delfini

Piazza del
Campitelli

G   H

Palazzo Altemps

- Aphrodite's Throne
- Galatian Soldier statue
- Courtyard loggia
- Statue of Orestes and Electra embracing in a fond farewell

TIPS

- A combined ticket is available, which includes entry to the Palazzo Altemps, Palazzo Massimo alle Terme and other sights.
- Tickets can be prebooked at www.pierreci.it or call ☎ 06 3996 7700 (Mon–Sat).

This beautiful building epitomizes the best of Renaissance urban architecture, while its series of elegant rooms provides the perfect setting for some of the finest of Rome's Classical sculpture.

The building Rome's Museo Nazionale Romano (National Roman Museum) is housed in two superbly restored buildings; the Palazzo Massimo alle Terme (▷ 82–83) near the station and here in the Palazzo Altemps, whose odd-sounding name is the Italian corruption of the German name von Hohenemps. Mainly constructed in the 15th century, the building houses a series of charming and intimate rooms, many with vaulted ceilings. One gives access to a splendidly frescoed loggia overlooking the comings and goings of a harmonious inner courtyard. The best time to get

Clockwise from far left: a colossal exhibit, just one example from this top-class collection of Classical sculpture; statues watch over the Palazzo Altemps' peaceful courtyard; statuary exhibited in the arcades; the Painted Loggia on the upper floor

a sense of the building's history is as dusk falls, when the rooms and exhibits are imaginatively lit.

The collections The *palazzo* is home to the famous Ludovisi Collection, amassed by Cardinal Ludovico Ludovisi in the 17th century, as well as the Altemps collection, Egyptian antiques and portraits. Downstairs look for the *Tiber Apollo*, so called because it was found in the bed of the river in the late 19th century, and the two gigantic statues of Athena. Upstairs, the star of the collection, the Ludovisi Throne, is probably a Greek sculpture dedicated as a throne for Aphrodite, the protectress of sailors. From the 5th century BC, the delicate carving portrays the goddess rising from the sea foam, her draperies clinging to her. Do not miss the statue of the *Galatian Soldier and His Wife Committing Suicide*, apparently commissioned by Julius Caesar.

THE BASICS

✚ F5
✉ Piazza Sant' Apollinare 46
☎ 06 683 3759 or 06 3996 7700
🕐 Tue–Sun 9–7.45
🚌 30, 70, 87, 116, 492, 628 to Corso del Rinascimento
♿ Moderate

HIGHLIGHTS

- *Religion Succoured by Spain* (tagged 10) and *Salome* (29), Titian
- *Portrait of Two Venetians* (23), Raphael
- *Maddalena* (40) and *Rest on the Flight into Egypt* (42), Caravaggio
- *Birth and Marriage of the Virgin* (174/176), Giovanni di Paolo
- *Nativity* (200), Parmigianino
- *Salomé with Head of John the Baptist,* Titian
- *Innocent X,* Bernini
- *Battle of the Bay of Naples* (317), Pieter Brueghel the Elder
- *Penitant Magdalen,* Caravaggio

TIPS

- Use the audioguide, which is included in the price and helps make sense of what you're seeing.
- The paintings are not well lit so it is better to visit during the daylight hours.

One of Rome's largest palaces that contains one of the city's finest patrician art collections and offers the chance to admire some of the sumptuously decorated rooms of its private apartments.

A dynasty Little in the bland exterior of the Palazzo Doria Pamphilj prepares you for the glory of the beautiful rooms that lie within. The core of the building, which was built over the foundations of a storehouse dating back to ancient times, was erected in 1435, and it has withstood countless alterations and owners. The Doria Pamphilj dynasty was formed by yoking together the Doria, a famous Genoese seafaring clan, and the Pamphilj, a Rome-based patrician family. Most people come here for the paintings, but—when open—you can enjoy a guided tour around some

This magnificent palace is at the middle of lovely parkland laid out by Prince Camillo Pamphilj in the mid-17th century (left); inside the galleries are lavishly decorated with painted ceilings and statues and the walls adorned with golden framed mirrors (right)

of the private apartments in the 1,000-room palace. The most impressive is the Saletta Gialla (Yellow Room), decorated with 12 Gobelin tapestries made for Louis XV. In the Salone Verde (Green Room) are three important paintings: *Annunciation* by Filippo Lippi, *Portrait of a Gentleman* by Lorenzo Lotto and *Andrea Doria* (a famous admiral) by Sebastiano del Piombo.

Labyrinth of masterpieces The Pamphilj's art collection is displayed in ranks in four broad galleries. As the works are numbered, not tagged, it's worth investing in a guidebook from the ticket office. The finest painting is the famous Velázquez portrait, *Innocent X* (1650), a likeness that captured the pope's weak and suspicious nature so adroitly that Innocent is said to have lamented that it was 'too true, too true'.

THE BASICS

www.doriapamphilj.it

⊞ G5

✉ Via del Corso (entrance on Piazza del Collegio)

☎ 06 679 7323

🕐 Fri–Wed 10–5; plus evening concerts when apartments can be viewed

🚌 60, 62, 85, 95, 160, 492 and all other services to Piazza Venezia

♿ Good

💷 Gallery expensive. Apartments moderate

Pantheon

HIGHLIGHTS

- Façade inscription
- The pedimented portico
- Original Roman doors
- Marble interior and pavement
- Coffered dome and oculus
- Tomb of Raphael
- Royal tombs

TIP

- The Pantheon is often very crowded. To make the most of your visit, go on a week-day or early in the morning.

No other monument suggests the grandeur of ancient Rome as magnificently as this temple whose early conversion to a place of Christian worship has rendered it the most perfect of the city's ancient monuments.

Temple and church The greatest surviving complete Roman structure, built by Emperor Hadrian from AD118–28, the Pantheon replaced a temple of 27BC by Marcus Agrippa, son-in-law of Augustus. (Modestly, Hadrian retained the original inscription proclaiming it as Agrippa's work.) It became the church of Santa Maria ad Martyres in AD609 (the bones of martyrs were brought here from the Catacombs) and is now a shrine to Italy's 'immortals', including the artist Raphael and kings Vittore Emanuele II and Umberto I.

Clockwise from far left: visitors gaze in astonishment at the Pantheon's dome; Raphael's Tomb; Giacomo della Porta's fountain in Piazza della Rotonda; the sun pours through the opening in the Pantheon's roof; 16 massive Egyptian granite columns support the portico

An engineering marvel Massive and simple from the outside, the Pantheon is at its most breathtaking inside, where the scale, harmony and symmetry of the dome in particular are more apparent. The world's largest dome until 1882 (when it was surpassed in the English spa resort of Buxton), it has a diameter of 43.3m (142ft)—equal to its height from the floor. Weight and stresses were reduced by rows of coffers in the ceiling, and the use of progressively lighter materials from the base to the crown. The central oculus, 9m (30ft) in diameter and clearly intended to inspire meditation on the heavens above, lets light (and rain) fall onto the marble pavement far below. Take time to relax in one of Piazza della Rotanda's many cafés to enjoy and admire the exterior view of the Pantheon and the atmosphere of the lively piazza.

THE BASICS

🔲 F5
✉ Piazza della Rotonda
☎ 06 6830 0230
🕐 Mon–Sat 8.30–7.30, Sun 9–6, public holidays 9–1
🚌 116, 119 to Piazza della Rotonda or 40, 64, 70 and all other services to Largo di Torre Argentina
♿ Good
💶 Free

Piazza Campo de' Fiori

TOP 25

Vibrant market stalls surround the statue of Giordano Bruno in Campo de' Fiori

THE BASICS

➕ F6

✉ Piazza Campo de' Fiori

🕐 Market Mon–Sat 7–1.30

🚌 40, 46, 62, 64 to Corso Vittorio Emanuele II or H, 8, 46, 62, 64, 70, 87 to Largo di Torre Argentina

♿ Cobbled streets and some curbs around piazza

🎟 Free

HIGHLIGHTS

● Street market
● Wine bar Vineria Reggio (▷ 60)
● Statue of Giordano Bruno marking where the philosopher was martyred for heresy in 1600
● Piazza della Cancelleria
● Palazzo Pio Righetti
● Santa Maria dell'Orazione e Morte: church door decorated in stone skulls
● The inscription on 'new' La Terrina (Tureen) fountain: Do well and let them talk'

There is nowhere more relaxing in Rome to sit and watch the world go by than Campo de' Fiori, a lovely old piazza whose fruit, vegetable and fish market makes it one of the liveliest and most vivid corners of the old city.

Ancient square Campo de' Fiori, or the 'Field of Flowers', was turned in the Middle Ages from a meadow facing the ancient Theatre of Pompey (55BC; now Palazzo Pio Righetti) into one of the city's most exclusive residential and business districts. By the 15th century it was surrounded by busy inns and bordellos, some run by the infamous courtesan Vannozza Catanei, mistress of the Borgia pope Alexander VI. By 1600 it had also become a place of execution; as testified by the cowled statue of Giordana Bruno (or 'Gordon Brown', as the name translates).

Present day Just sit back and soak up the atmosphere. Students, foreigners, locals and tramps mingle with the market vendors shouting their wares, while the cafés, bars and the wonderfully dingy wine bar at No. 15, the Vineria, will have you relishing the street life. One block south lies Piazza Farnese, dominated by the Palazzo Farnese, a Renaissance masterpiece partly designed by Michelangelo and begun in 1516. It is now home to the French Embassy. One block west is the Palazzo della Cancelleria (1485), once the papal chancellery. The nearby Via Giulia, Via dei Baullari, the busy Via dei Cappellari and Via del Pellegrino are all wonderful streets to explore.

TOP 25

Piazza Navona

Piazza di Spagna may be more elegant and Campo de' Fiori more vivid, but Piazza Navona, with its atmospheric echoes of a 2,000-year history, is a glorious place to amble or stop for a drink at a sun-drenched table.

Shaping history Piazza Navona owes its unmistakable elliptical shape to a stadium and racetrack built here in AD86 by Emperor Domitian. From the Circus Agonalis—the stadium for athletic games—comes the piazza's present name, rendered in medieval Latin as *in agone*, and then in Rome's strangulated dialect as *'n 'agona*. The stadium was used until well into the Middle Ages for festivals and competitions. The square owes its present appearance to its rebuilding by Pope Innocent X in 1644.

Around the piazza Bernini's spirited Fontana dei Quattro Fiumi (1651), the 'Fountain of the Four Rivers', dominates. Unveiled in 1651, it has four figures that represent the four rivers of Paradise (the Nile, Ganges, Danube and Plate), and the four 'corners' of the world (Africa, Asia, Europe and America). On the west side is the baroque Sant' Agnese (1652–57), its façade designed by Borromini. Beside it stands the Palazzo Pamphilj, commissioned by Innocent X and now the Brazilian Embassy. Further afield, San Luigi dei Francesi is famous for three superlative Caravaggio paintings, and Santa Maria della Pace for a cloister by Bramante and Raphael's frescoes of the four *Sybils*.

THE BASICS

🔲 F5
✉ Piazza Navona
Ⓢ Spagna
🚌 30, 70, 51, 87, 116, 492, 628 to Corso del Rinascimento or 40, 46, 62, 64 to Corso Vittorio Emanuele II

HIGHLIGHTS

- Fontana dei Quattro Fiumi
- Fontana del Moro (south)
- Fontana del Nettuno (north)
- Palazzo Pamphilj
- San Luigi dei Francesi (Via Santa Giovanna d' Arco)
- Santa Maria dell'Anima (Via della Pace)

Santa Maria sopra Minerva

Soaring Gothic arches (left); Bernini's elephant (middle); Tomb of St. Catherine (right)

THE BASICS

✚ G5
✉ Piazza della Minerva 42
☎ 06 679 3926
🕐 Mon–Sat 7–7, Sun 8–7 (10–6 in winter)
🚌 H, 8, 30, 40, 46, 62, 64, 70, 81, 87 to Lago di Torre Argentina or 119 to Piazza della Rotonda
♿ Stepped access to church
🎫 Free

HIGHLIGHTS

● Plaques marking the height of the Tiber floods, which plagued the city between 1422 and 1870, on the side of the building
● The church's star-spangled blue ceiling
● Relics of St. Catherine of Siena, and preserved room in sacristy where she died
● The headquarters of the Dominican preaching order, which serves the church, to the left of the building
● The 6th century BC Egyptian obelisk above Bernini's elephant, known as Pulcin della Minerva (Minerva's chick)

Remarkable in having retained many Gothic features despite Rome's love for the baroque, behind its plain façade Santa Maria sopra Minerva is a cornucopia of tombs, paintings and Renaissance sculpture.

Florentine influences Originally founded in the 8th century over ruins of a temple to Minerva, the church was built in 1280 to a design by two Florentine Dominican monks who fashioned it on their own church, Santa Maria Novella. Before entering the church, notice its strange but charming statue of an elephant supporting a 6th-century BC Egyptian obelisk in the piazza outside. It was designed by Bernini in the 17th century.

Inside The interior of the church abounds with beautiful works such as the Cappella Carafa (whose fine porch is attributed to Giuliano da Maiano), and Michelangelo's calm statue *The Risen Christ* (1521), left of the high altar. Filippino Lippi painted the celebrated frescos *St. Thomas Aquinas* and the *Assumption* (1488–93). Among other sculptures are the tombs of Francesco Tornabuoni (1480) and that of Giovanni Alberini, the latter decorated with reliefs of Hercules (15th century). Both are attributed to Mino da Fiesole. Other works include Fra Angelico's tomb slab (1455); the tombs of Medici popes Clement VII and Leo X (1536) by Antonio da Sangallo the Younger; and Bernini's monument to Maria Raggi (1643). St. Catherine of Siena, one of Italy's patron saints, is buried beneath the high altar.

COLONNA DI MARCO AURELIO

The Column of Marcus Aurelius (AD180–96) was built to celebrate Aurelius's military triumphs over hostile north European tribes. It is composed of 27 separate drums of Carrara marble welded into a seamless whole, and is done with a continuous spiral of bas-reliefs commemorating episodes from the victorious campaigns. Aurelius is depicted no fewer than 59 times, though curiously never actually in battle. At the top of the 50m (140ft) structure stands a statue of St. Paul who replaced the 60th depiction of Aurelius in 1589.

✚ G5 ✉ Piazza Colonna, Via del Corso ⏰ Always open 🚇 Barberini 🚌 62, 63, 85, 95, 117, 119 and all routes to Via del Corso 💷 Free

CRYPTA BALBI

This museum, part of the Museo Nazionale Romano, contains part of a theatre built in 13BC, along with a rich collection of objects to illustrate social, economic and urban planning changes from ancient times, through the Middle Ages up to the present day. Two other sections have displays of vases, glassware, mosaics and other items dating from between the 5th and 8th centuries.

✚ G6 ✉ Via delle Botteghe Oscure 31 ⏰ 06 3996 7700 ⏰ Tue–Sun 9–7.45 🚇 Colosseum 🚌 30,40, 46, 62, 64, 70, 492, 628, 780, 787, 916 to Largo di Torre Argentina 💷 Expensive

FONTANA DELLE TARTARUGHE

This tiny fountain (1581–84) is one of Rome's most delightful sights, thanks to the tortoises, probably added by Bernini in 1658 (the current bronze sculptures are copies).

✚ F6 ✉ Piazza Mattei 🚌 H, 8, 63, 630, 780 to Via Arenula or 30, 70, 87, 116 and other services to Largo di Torre Argentina

MUSEO NAZIONALE DELLE PASTE ALIMENTARI

www.pastainmuseum.it

This unusual museum closed down temporarily in late 2007, leaving a big hole in the schedules of devotees of Italy's preferred food. At the time of

Colonna di Marco Aurelio

Detail of the Fontana delle Tartarughe showing a boy reaching up to a tortoise

writing it isn't known when or where it will reopen, having left its premises in Piazza Scanderberg. Its novel presentation of the evolution of pasta has been missed. Check the website for news of reopening.

✚ H5 ⏱ 06 699 1119 💰 Expensive

MUSEO DEL PALAZZO VENEZIA

Built in 1455 for Pietro Barbo (later Pope Paul II), and one of the first Renaissance palaces, the former Venetian Embassy became the property of the state in 1916; Mussolini harangued the crowds from the balconies. The museum hosts visiting exhibitions and a fine permanent collection that includes Renaissance paintings, sculpture, armour, ceramics, silverware and objets d'art.

✚ G6 ✉ Palazzo Venezia, Via del Plebiscito 118 ☎ 06 6999 4318; reservations 06 328101 ⏱ Tue–Sun 8.30–7.30; closed holidays 🚌 All services to Piazza Venezia 💶 Moderate

PALAZZO SPADA

This pretty *palazzo*, with a creamy stucco façade (1556–62), has four rooms where you can admire the 17th- and 18th-century Spada family paintings. Cardinal Spada is portrayed by Guido Reni; there's a fine Borromini *Perspective* and works by Albrecht Dürer, Andrea del Sarto and others.

✚ F6 ✉ Piazza Capo di Ferro 13–Vicolo del Polverone 15b ☎ 06 687 4893/4896 or 06 683 2409 ⏱ Tue–Sat 8.30–7.30 🚌 H, 8, 63, 630, 780 to Via Arenula 💶 Moderate

SANT'AGOSTINO

One of the first Renaissance churches in Rome, Sant'Agostino still maintains its Latin-cross plan with apse, chapels and dome. Even if 19th-century additions have ruined its elegance, it is still worth visiting to see the works of Caravaggio, Raphael and other fine artists. The first chapel on the left contains Caravaggio's magnificent *Madonna di Loreto*.

✚ F5 ✉ Piazza di Sant'Agostino ⏱ Daily 8–12, 4.30–7.30 🚌 116 to Via Zanardelli; 30, 40, 46, 62, 63, 64, 70 to Largo di Torre Argentina; 30, 70, 87, 130, 186 to Corso del Rinascimento

The perspectival gallery in the Palazzo Spada

Sant'Agostino, one of Rome's earliest Renaissance churches

The Medieval City

Explore the tangle of streets around some of Rome's most popular piazzas, taking in some of the best-known sights along the way.

DISTANCE: 2.5km (1.5 miles)   **ALLOW:** 2 hours

START

CAMPO DE' FIORI (▷ 48)
🚇 F6 🚌 40, 60, 62, 116 and other services to Corso Vittorio Emanuele II

① Walk east on Via dei Giubbonari and take the third right, Via d'Arco del Monte. Continue down Via dei Pettinari and right through the arch into Via Giulia.

② Take the fourth right opposite the church with the skull-adorned façade and admire Piazza Farnese before following Vicolo Gallo back into Campo de' Fiori.

③ Take Via dei Cappellari out of the campo and go left on Via del Pellegrino and then right on Via dei Banchi Vecchi. Cross Corso Vittorio Emanuele II into Via Banco Santo Spirito, then go immediately right on Via del Governo Vecchio.

④ Continue to the end to visit Piazza Navona (▷ 49). Or explore the tangle of lovely streets to the west of this piazza by turning sixth left on Vicolo del Corallo to Piazza del Fico.

END

PIAZZA DELLA ROTONDA
🚇 F5 🚌 116, 116T to Piazza della Rotonda

⑧ Otherwise, go north on Via della Scrofa, then right on Via Stelletta to Piazza Campo Marzio. Turn right on Via Uffici del Vicario, then right on Via Maddalena to Piazza della Rotonda.

⑦ Take the southeast corner of Piazza Sant'Apollinare into Piazza Sant' Agostino to see the church (▷ 52). Go past the church and left into Via della Scrofa. Turn right on Via della Scrofa and cross Largo Toniolo to see the Caravaggios in San Luigi dei Francesi.

⑥ Turn left to look at antiques shops on Via dei Coronari, or right and cross Piazza di Tor Sanguigna, and then left into Piazza Sant' Apollinare, to the Palazzo Altemps (▷ 42–43).

⑤ Take Via della Fossa east out of Piazza del Fico and turn left on Via del Parione, then left on Vicolo delle Volpe to Via dei Coronari.

Shopping

AI MONASTERI

This unusual, large and rather dark old shop sells the products of seven Italian monasteries, from honeys, wines, natural preserves and liqueurs to herbal cures and elixirs.
⊞ F5 ✉ Piazza Cinque Lune 76 (corner of Corso del Rinascimento) ☎ 06 6880 2783 🕔 Fri– Wed 9–1, 4.30–7.30, Thu 9–1; closed 1st week of Sep

ANTICA LIBRERIA CROCE

This primarily Italian bookshop, with some titles in English, specializes in books on all aspects of Classical and contemporary art and photography. Over two floors; from time to time exhibitions are held here.
⊞ F6 ✉ Corso Vittorio Emanuele II 56, corner of Corso del Rinascimento ☎ 06 6880 2269 🕔 Tue–Sat 10–8, Sun 10–1.30, 4–8.30

BASSETTI

Central shop with a dazzling collection of quality Italian silks and other luxurious fabrics, plus everyday materials.
⊞ E5 ✉ Corso Vittorio Emanuele II 73 ☎ 06 689 2326 🕔 Tue–Sat 9–7.30 (Jul–end Aug 9–1, 4–6), Mon 4–6 (hours can vary)

CAMPO DE' FIORI

This picturesque market is in a pretty, central square. Fruit and vegetables dominate, but you can also buy fish,
flowers and beans.
⊞ F6 ✉ Piazza Campo de' Fiori 🕔 Mon–Sat 7am–1.30pm

CARTOLERIA PANTHEON

Beautiful handcrafted notebooks, exquisite stationery and a wide variety of objects covered in marbled paper.

SHOPPING AREAS

Most of the city's quality and specialty shops are concentrated in specific areas. Via Condotti and its surrounding grid of streets (Via Frattina, Via Borgognona and Via Bocca di Leone) contain most of the big names in men's and women's fashion, accessories, jewellery and luxury goods. In nearby Via del Babuino and Via Margutta, the emphasis is on top antiques, paintings, sculpture and modern glassware and lighting. Via della Croce, which runs south from Piazza di Spagna, is known for its food shops, while Via del Corso, which bisects the northern half of central Rome, is home to bargain mid-range clothes, shoes and accessories shops. For inexpensive shops visit Via del Tritone and Via Nazionale. Nice areas to browse for antiques, even if you are not buying, include Via Giulia, Via dei Coronari, Via dell'Orso, Via dei Soldati and Via del Governo Vecchio.

⊞ F5 ✉ Via della Rotonda 15 ☎ 06 687 5313 🕔 Mon–Sat 10.30–7.30, Sun 1–7.30

CULTI

A shop near Piazza Navona packed with linens, well-designed kitchen utensils, plates, glasses, vases, towels, sheets and a host of other articles for the home.
⊞ F5 ✉ Via della Vetrina 16a ☎ 06 683 2180 🕔 Tue–Sat 10–1.30, 4–7.30, Mon 4–7.30

ENOTECA AL GOCCETTO

Wines from all over Italy are sold in this old bishop's *palazzo*, complete with original floors and wooden ceiling.
⊞ E5 ✉ Via dei Banchi Vecchi 14 ☎ 06 686 4268 🕔 Mon–Sat 11.30–2, 7–11, closed 3 weeks in Aug

ETHIC

Individual Italian chainstore with good midrange fashion just east of Campo de' Fiori.
⊞ F6 ✉ Piazza Benedetto Cairoli 11–12 ☎ 06 6830 1063 🕔 Tue–Sat 10–8, Sun–Mon 12–8

FABINDIA

www.fabindia.it
Facing the Ponte Sant'Angelo is this delightful emporium selling Indian fabrics, scarves and garments, all handwoven and made in Indian villages. The company is devoted to developing fair and

equitable relationships with the producers. The style is both traditional and more contemporary.
E5 ✉ Via del Banco di Santo Spirito 40 ☎ 06 6889 1230 🕐 Mon–Sat 10–1.30, 3–7.30

FELTRINELLI

An Italy-wide bookshop chain with well-designed shelves displaying a broad range of Italian titles, and usually a reasonable choice of French-German- and English-language books.
F6 ✉ Largo di Torre Argentina 7–10 ☎ 06 6866 3001 🕐 Mon–Sat 9–8, Sun 10–1.30, 4–7.30
G3 ✉ Via del Babuino 39–41 ☎ 06 3600 1873 🕐 Mon–Sat 9–8, Sun 10–1.30, 4–7.30
J4 ✉ Via Vittorio Emanuele II Orlando 78–81/84 ☎ 06 484 430 or 06 487 0171 🕐 Mon–Sat 9–8, Sun 10–1.30, 4–7.30

HOUSE & KITCHEN

More traditional than Spazio Sette (▷ below). This shop sells a range of household goods, notably a selection of kitchen utensils and kitchenware.
G6 ✉ Via del Plebiscito 103 ☎ 06 679 4208 🕐 Mon–Sat 9.30–8, Sun 10.30–2.30, 4–8; closed Sun in Jul and Aug

MARIA GRAZIA LUFFARELLI

Bright watercolour landscapes of hills, sea and sun. Prices range from very low to moderate for original works by the eponymous artist. Also on sale is a lovely range of Rome watercolour reproductions in postcard format, plus prints of Luffarelli's work mounted on brightly painted tables.
E5 ✉ Via dei Banchi Vecchi 29 ☎ 06 683 2494 🕐 Mon–Sat 11–8

MONDELLO OTTICA

www.mondelloottica.it
Eyewear with a difference: This minimalist boutique has regular installations by local artists. Prices may be higher than average, but the glasses are superlative in quality and sheer chic. Prescription glasses can be made within a day.
E5 ✉ Vial del Pellegrino 98 ☎ 06 686 1955 🕐 Tue–Sat 9.30–1, 4–7.30

GIFTS WITH A TWIST

For a souvenir with a difference, visit the extraordinary shops on Via dei Cestari, just south of the Pantheon, which specialize in all sorts of religious clothes, candles and vestments. Crucifixes, rosaries, statues of saints and other religious souvenirs can be found in shops on Via di Porta Angelica near the Vatican. Alternatively, visit the Farmacia Santa Maria della Scala (✉ Piazza Santa Maria della Scala), an 18th-century monastic pharmacy that sells herbal remedies.

ORNAMENTUM

A beautiful shop selling silks and other sumptuous fabrics, tassels, brocades and other furnishing accessories.
E5 ✉ Via dei Coronari 227 ☎ 06 687 6849 🕐 Tue–Fri 9–1, 4–7.30, Sat 9–1, Mon 4–7.30; closed Aug

PIAZZA COPPELLE

This tiny, attractive local food market is an oasis among the cars and tourists. Close to the Pantheon.
F5 ✉ Piazza Coppelle 🕐 Mon–Sat 6am–2pm

POGGI

Vivid pigments, lovely papers and exquisitely soft brushes have been on sale at Poggi's since 1825. The second shop almost opposite sells high-quality paper.
G5 ✉ Via del Gesù 74–5 ☎ 06 678 4477 🕐 Mon–Sat 9–1, 4–7.30
G5 ✉ Via Piè di Marmo 40–1 ☎ 06 6830 8014 🕐 Mon–Fri 9–1, 4–7.30, Sat 9–1

SPAZIO SETTE

Housed in a 17th-century cardinal's palace, this is one of the few stores in Rome that will make even the most hardened shopper salivate over furnishings for the kitchen, living room and bathroom.
F6 ✉ Via dei Barbieri 7 ☎ 06 686 947 🕐 Tue–Sat 9.30–1, 3.30–7.30, Mon 3.30–7.30

Entertainment and Nightlife

ANIMA

At the heart of a small buzzing nightlife area, Anima is a welcoming bar and club that plays an eclectic assortment of music and attracts a clientele of all ages and types. 🔼 F5 🖂 Via Santa Maria dell'Anima 57 ☎ 06 6889 2806 🕐 Daily 6pm–4am 🚌 30, 70, 87 and other services to Corso del Rinascimento or Corso Vittorio Emanuele II

ASSOCIAZIONE MUSICALE ROMANA

www.assmusrom.it
Stages a summer season of chamber recitals at a number of venues, including the French Academy in the Villa Medici. 🔼 G3 🖂 Via Gregorio 216 ☎ 06 3936 6322

BEVITORIA NAVONA

Friendlier and more intimate than most larger bars on Piazza Navona. Primarily a wine bar (the cellar is part of Domitian's former stadium). 🔼 F5 🖂 Piazza Navona 72 ☎ 06 6880 1022 🕐 Daily 10am–1am 🚌 46, 62, 64 to Corso Vittorio Emanuele II or 30, 70, 81, 87, 116 to Corso del Rinascimento

CUL DE SAC

Rome's original informal wine bar near Piazza Navona with pine tables and a big marble bar. More than 1,400 wines, plus snacks, light meals and cheese and salami from every region in Italy. 🔼 F5 🖂 Piazza Pasquino 73 ☎ 06 6880 1094 🕐 Daily 12–4pm, 6–12.30 🚌 46, 62, 64 to Corso Vittorio Emanuele II

ENOTECA PICCOLA

Intimate wine bar close to Piazza Navona, ideal for a romantic interlude. 🔼 E5 🖂 Via del Governo Vecchio 74–5 ☎ 06 6880 1746 🕐 Tue–Sun 12–3.30, 7–1 🚌 46, 62, 64 to Corso Vittorio Emanuele II

IL GONFALONE

A small but prestigious company that hosts chamber music and other small-scale recitals. 🔼 E5 🖂 Oratorio del Gonfalone, Via del Gonfalone 32a; Information 🖂 Vicolo della Scimmia 1b ☎ 06 687 5952 🕐 Concerts Oct–Jun, call for times; box office Mon–Fri 9am–1pm, day of concert 9–9 🚌 46, 62, 64 to Corso Vittorio Emanuele II or 23, 116, 280 to Lungotevere di Sangallo

SOCIÉTÉ LUTÈCE

This new bar buzzes at aperitivo hour (around 7pm) with gargantuan snacks. The clientele is boho cool, laid-back and the music good—ideal for people-watching as the beautiful spill out into the small piazza. 🔼 F5 🖂 Piazza di Montevecchio, 17 ☎ 06 683 01472 🕐 Tue–Sat 6.30pm–2am 🚌 Many services to Corso Vittorio Emanuele II

TRINITY COLLEGE

This is one of the better historic pubs in the centro storico. Its serves inexpensive food as well as Guinness. 🔼 G5 🖂 Via del Collegio Romano ☎ 06 678 6472 🕐 Daily noon–3am 🚌 62, 63, 85, 95, 117, 119 to Via del Corso and all services to Piazza Venezia

LA VINERIA REGGIO

The quainter side of nighttime drinking. Fusty and old-fashioned inside, with characters to match; tables on the city's most evocative square. Also try the popular Drunken Ship pub virtually next door. 🔼 F6 🖂 Campo de' Fiori 15 ☎ 06 6880 3268 🕐 Mon–Sat 8.30am–2am, Sun 5pm–2am 🚌 46, 62, 64 to Corso Vittorio Emanuele II, 116 to Via Baullari or 70, 81, 87 to Corso del Rinascimento

---

APERITIVI TIME

The great Torinese predilection for the predinner 'aperitivo' has arrived in the Eternal City. Hailing from Turin, gallery and bar-owners Luca Conzato and Riccardo Ronchi have highly successfully introduced the idea to Rome with their neo-boho bar Société Lutèce (▷ above). Arrive after 7pm and you can feast or graze on generous snacks of pasta, cold meats, couscous, cheese and much more all for the price of a glass of wine. Other very popular aperitivo bars such as Etabli (🖂 Vicolo delle Vacche 9) are popping up all the time.

Restaurants

L'ALTRO MASTAI (€€€)

Young chef Fabio Baldassare's Michelin-starred restaurant is a temple to gastronomy. This is among Rome's top dining experiences set in both opulent and intimate neo-Pompian surroundings. The cuisine is creative Italian, the service is impeccable and the bill demands deep pockets.

➕ E5 ✉ Via Giraud 53 ☎ 06 6830 1296 🕐 Tue–Sat 7.30–11.30pm; closed lunch, one week in Jan and Aug 🚌 Many services to Corso Vittorio Emanuele II

ANTICA BIRRERIA PERONI (€)

Ideal for a simple lunch or dinner. Original art nouveau interior and a large beer hall.

➕ G5 ✉ Via di San Marcello 19 ☎ 06 679 5310 🕐 Mon–Sat 12–12 🚌 63, 75, 81, 84, 87 and all other buses to Piazza Venezia

IL BACARO (€€€)

www.ilbacaro.com

Tiny but gracious restaurant. It can be noisy, but the light, modern pan-Italian cooking is great. Must reserve ahead.

➕ F5 ✉ Via degli Spagnoli 27, near Piazza delle Coppelle ☎ 06 686 4110 or 06 687 2554 🕐 Mon–Sat 8am–11.30pm; closed Aug 🚇 Spagna 🚌 119

BAR DELLA PACE (€)

Extremely trendy bar, which is quieter by day, when you can eat outside or enjoy the 19th-century mahogany interior.

➕ F5 ✉ Via della Pace 3, off Piazza Navona ☎ 06 686 1216 🕐 Daily 9am–2am (Mon 4–2) 🚌 30, 70, 87, 116 to Corso del Rinascimento

CAFFÈ FARNESE (€)

Quieter and more elegant than the bars on the nearby Campo de' Fiori. Serves cakes, ice creams and light snacks as well as drinks. Also tables on the cobbled street.

➕ E6 ✉ Via dei Baullari 106–7, at Piazza Farnese ☎ 06 6880 2125 🕐 Daily 7am–2am 🚌 8, 46, 62, 64

CICCIA BOMBA (€€)

An excellent option amid the plethora of restaurants around Piazza Navona. Tastefully decorated sprinkled with antiques, efficient service, and good Roman food at good prices for this area.

➕ E5 ✉ Via dell Governo Vecchio 76 ☎ 06 6880 2108 🕐 Thu–Tue 12.30–3, 7.30–11.30; closed 2 weeks in Aug 🚌 All services to Corso del Rinascimento or Corso Vittorio Emanuele II

IL CONVIVIO TROIANI (€€€)

www.ilconviviotroiani.com

The Troiani brothers from Italy's Marche region have created a tranquil little restaurant with a reputation for innovative and subtle tasting modern dishes.

➕ F4 ✉ Vicolo dei Soldati 31 ☎ 06 686 9432 🕐 Mon–Sat dinner only 8–10.30; closed 13–17 Aug 🚌 30, 70, 87, 116, 492 to Corso del Rinascimento

DA BAFFETTO (€)

A tiny, hole-in-the-wall pizzeria that has retained its atmosphere and low prices. Thin, crisp pizzas fired in a traditional oven are the specialty. Very popular so expect to wait for a table.

➕ E5 ✉ Via del Governo

THE MENU

Starters are called antipasti; first course (soup, pasta or risotto) is *il primo*; and main meat and fish dishes are *il secondo*. Salads (*insalata*) and vegetables (*contorni*) are ordered (and often eaten) separately. Desserts are *dolci*, with cheese (*formaggio*) or fruit (*frutta*) to follow. If no menu card is offered, ask for *la lista* or *il menù*. A set-price menu (*un menù turistico*) may seem good value, but portions are usually small and the food is invariably poor—usually just spaghetti with a tomato sauce, followed by a piece of chicken and fruit.

Vecchio 114 ☎ 06 686 1617
🕐 Daily 6.30 –1am; closed
Aug 🚌 46, 62, 64 to Corso
Vittorio Emanuele II

DA FRANCESCO (€)

A simple restaurant near
Piazza Navona, which over
the years has never lost its
appeal, thanks to a warm,
friendly atmosphere, good
food and low prices. No
reservations so arrive early
to be sure of a place.
➕ E5 ✉ Piazza del Fico 29
☎ 06 686 4009
🕐 Wed–Mon 12–3, 7–1, Tue
7pm–1am 🚌 64 and other
services to Chiesa Nuova on
Corso Vittorio Emanuele II

DITIRAMBO (€€)

www.ristoranteditirambo.it
Downtown *trattoria* that
far transcends the tourist
menu, even satisfying the
difficult-to-please *bel
mondo* of Rome. The
kitchen uses organic
ingredients, and produces
homemade bread, pasta
and desserts.
Reservations essential.
➕ F6 ✉ Piazza della
Cancelleria 72 ☎ 06 687
1626 🕐 Tue–Sun 1–3,
7.30–11.30, Mon
8pm–11.30pm; closed Aug
🚌 46, 62, 64, 87, 116, 492 to
Corso Vittorio Emanuele II

DUR FILETTARO A
SANTA BARBARA (€)

At this tiny place with
Formica tables you wash
down cod with plenty of
beer or crisp local wine.
➕ F6 ✉ Largo dei Librari
88, off Via dei Giubbonari
☎ 06 686 4018 🕐 Mon–Sat

5.30–11; closed Aug and 1
week Dec–Jan 🚌 H, 8, 63,
630, 780 to Via Arenula

GELATERIA DELLA
PALMA (€)

A big, brash place just
behind the Pantheon near
the Trevi Fountain. Cakes
and chocolates, plus more
than 100 varieties of ice
cream—many of them a
little wild.
➕ F5 ✉ Via della
Maddalena 20 ☎ 06 6880
6752 🕐 Daily 8am–midnight
🚌 116 to Piazza della Rotonda

GIOLITTI (€)

For years Giolitti was the
king of Roman ice cream.
Standards have slipped
slightly, but the ice cream
is still excellent value.
➕ F5 ✉ Via Uffici del
Vicario 40 ☎ 06 699 1243
🕐 Mon–Fri, Sun

<table>
<tr><td>THE BILL</td></tr>
</table>

The bill (check), *il conto*,
usually includes extras such
as *servizio* (service).
Iniquitous cover charges
(*pane e coperto*) have now
been outlawed, but some
restaurants still try to get
round the regulations. Only
pay for bread (*pane*) if you
have asked for it. Proper
receipts—not a scrawled piece
of paper—must be given by
law. If you receive a scrap of
paper, which is more likely in
a pizzeria, and have doubts
about the total, be sure to
ask for a proper receipt (*una
fattura* or *una ricevuta*).

7am–12.30am, Sat 7am–2am
🚌 119 to Piazza della Rotonda
or 62, 80, 81, 85, 95, 117, 119,
160, 175 and other services to
Corso del Rinascimento

GRAPPOLO D'ORO
(€€)

Unspoiled *trattoria* loved
by locals and foreign resi-
dents for decades. The
menu has *pasta all'
Amatriciana* and *scalop-
pine* any way you like.
➕ F6 ✉ Piazza della
Cancelleria 80 ☎ 06 689
7080 🕐 Daily 1–3,
7.30–11.30; closed lunch Tue–
Thu in winter 🚌 46, 62, 64
to Corso Vittorio Emanuele II

'GUSTO (€€)

A chic, modern restaurant
on two levels where you
can eat pizzas, salads and
other light meals down-
stairs or fuller meals
upstairs. There is also a
good kitchenware shop.
➕ F3 ✉ Piazza Augusto
Imperatore 9 ☎ 06 322 6273
🕐 Daily 1–3, 7.30–1 🚌 117,
119 to Via del Corso

LATTERIA DEL
GALLO (€)

Marble tables and 1940s
decor in this, Rome's last
old-style 'milk bar'. Try the
big, sticky cakes and
steaming hot chocolate.
➕ E6 ✉ Vicolo del Gallo 4
☎ 06 686 5091 🕐 Thu–Tue
8.30–2, 5–midnight 🚌 46,
62, 64 to Corso Vittorio
Emanuele II

L'EAU VIVE (€€)

Expect a bizarre but heav-
enly dining experience

here. Predominantly French food is served by nuns. Politicians, celebrities and locals come to enjoy the food and the beautiful 16th-century frescoed dining rooms.
🚇 F5 ✉ Via Monterone 85 ☎ 06 6880 1095 🕐 Mon–Sat 12.30–3.30, 7.30–10; closed Aug 🚌 8, 46, 62, 63, 64, 70, 87, 186, 492 to Largo di Torre Argentina

IL PAGLIACCIO (€€€)
Inventive chef Anthony Genovese was awarded his Michelin star in 2007, and this gourmet experience continues to be a superb combination of Mediterranean, Oriental and traditional cuisine. The smart and small restaurant is splendidly run.
🚇 E5 ✉ Via dei Banchi Vecchi 129 ☎ 06 6880 9595 🕐 Wed–Sat lunch and dinner; Tue dinner

LA ROSETTA (€€€)
An exclusive fish and seafood restaurant whose popularity means reservations are a must.
🚇 F5 ✉ Via della Rosetta 8–9 ☎ 06 686 1002 🕐 Mon–Sat 1–3, 8–11.30; closed 10–30 Aug 🚌 119 to Piazza della Rotonda or 70, 87, 90 to Corso del Rinascimento

SALOTTO 42 (€)
Warm and relaxed place for drinks or light meals, especially during the day and in the evening a stylish cocktail bar.
🚇 G5 ✉ Piazza di Pietro 42 ☎ 06 678 5804 🕐 Tue–Sun

10am–2am (earlier on Sun) 🚌 C3, 62, 63, 85, 91

SANT' EUSTACHIO (€)
Excellent coffee served in a pleasant interior and tables outside. One of Rome's best.
🚇 F5 ✉ Piazza Sant' Eustachio 82 ☎ 06 6880 2048 🕐 Daily 8.30am–1am 🚌 119 to Piazza della Rotonda or 30, 70, 87, 116 to Corso del Rinascimento

LA TAZZA D'ORO (€)
The Cup of Gold sells only coffee; probably the city's best espresso and *granita di caffé* (coffee ice).
🚇 G5 ✉ Via degli Orfani 84 ☎ 06 678 9792 🕐 Mon–Sat 7am–8pm 🚌 119 to Piazza della Rotonda or 30, 70, 87, 116, 186 to Corso del Rinascimento

THIEN KIM (€)
More adventurous Romans have been

visiting this calm and courteous restaurant for Vietnamese food since 1976. Very good value.
🚇 E6 ✉ Via Giulia 201 ☎ 06 6830 7832 🕐 Mon–Sat 7.30–10.30 🚌 46, 64 to Corso Vittorio Emanuele II

TRE SCALINI (€)
Known for its chocolate-studded *tartufo* (the best chocolate-chip ice cream) served with cream.
🚇 F5 ✉ Piazza Navona 28–32 ☎ 06 6880 1996 🕐 Daily Thu–Tue 8am–1am 🚌 30, 70, 87, 116 and other services to Corso del Rinascimento

TUCCI (€)
You can sit here for hours facing Bernini's Fontana dei Quattro Fiumi.
🚇 F5 ✉ Piazza Navona 94–100 ☎ 06 686 1547 🕐 Wed–Mon 8.30am–12.30am 🚌 46, 62, 64 to Corso Vittorio Emanuele II or 30, 70, 87, 116 to Corso del Rinascimento

VINERIA REGGIO GIORGIO (€)
The oldest wine bar on the Campo run by the same proprietor for 44 years, splendid for soaking up the atmosphere from tables spilling onto the street. Sandwiches and snacks are complemented by fine wines.
🚇 F5 ✉ Campo de' Fiori 15 ☎ 06 6880 3268 🕐 Mon–Sat 8.30am–2am 🚌 Many servcies to Corso Vittorio Emanuele II or Largo di Torre Argentina

CENTRAL ROME RESTAURANTS

Trastevere—literally 'across the Tiber'—is Rome's working-class district, an enclave of appealing streets and leafy corners full of cafés, bars and restaurants, as well as a handful of churches and galleries.

5

6

7

8

9

Via degli Orti d'Alibert

Via delle Martellate

Via di San

Francesco di Sales

LUNGOTEVERE GIANICOLENSE

Ponte Mazzini

della

Lungara

Tevere

LUNGOTEVERE DELLA FARNESINA

Ponte Sisto

LUNGOTEV

LUNGOT D

Via dei Riari

Palazzo Corsini

Villa Farnesina

Monte Gianicolo

Passeggiata del

Viale delle Mura Aurelie

Piazzale G Garibaldi

Gianicolo

Orto Botanico

VIA GARIBALDI

Via della Scala

Santa Maria della Scala

Vicolo del Cinque

Via del

Piazza de' Renzi

Via della Renel

LUNGOT D

Vicolo del Cedro

S Egidio

Piazza di S Maria in Trastevere

Via del Moro

Porta S Pancrazio

Via di Porta San Pancrazio

San Pietro in Montorio

Santa Maria in Trastevere

VIA GARIBALDI

Via Goffredo Mameli

Via Luciano Manara

Via di San Francesco a R

TRASTEVERE

Piazza San Cosimato

Via N d Grande

0   250 m

0   250 yds

D   **E**

ARENULA

Via Portico d'Ottavia

GHETTO

Via Catalana

Via delle Zoccolette

DEI VALLATI

LUNGOTEVERE DEI CENCI

VIA

Piazza
Monte
Savello

Monte Capitolino

VIA DEL TEATRO DI MARCELLO

Santa Nicola
in Carcere

PONTE
GARIBALDI

Isola
Tiberina

LUNGOT DELL' ANGUILLARA

LUNGOTEVERE DEI PIERLEONI

VIA LUIGI PETROSELLI

SANZIO

Piazza
G G Belli

San Bartolomeo
all' Isola

PONTE
PALATINO

Tempio della
Fortuna Virilis

Via

Belli
della

Lungaretta

Via dei salumi

Tempio
di Vesta

Piazza di
S Anastasia

San
Crisogono

Piazza
Sidney
Sonnino

Via dei Genovesi

Piazza Bocca
della Verità

Santa Maria
in Cosmedin

Mastai

Via S M
in Cappella

Via del

RIPA

VIA DEL CIRCO MASSIMO

Piazza
Mastai

Santa Cecilia
in Trastevere

LUNGOTEVERE

AVENTINO

Clivo de

Via
della
Luce

Via
Anicia

Via dei
Porto

AVENTINO

Via di San Michele

PORTO DI RIPA GRANDE

Clivo de Publicii

Tevere

Sabina

Santa
Sabina

Via di Santa Sabina

S Alessio

F

G

Santa Maria in Trastevere

HIGHLIGHTS

● Romanesque campanile
● Façade mosaics
● Portico
● Ceiling, by Domenichino
● Cosmati marble pavement
● Wall tabernacle by Mino del Reame (central nave)
● Byzantine gold mosaics in upper and lower apse
● The nave's Roman columns; some from the Terme di Caracalla
● *Madonna della Clemenza* in Cappella Altemps
● Cappella Avila: baroque chapel

TIP

● Visit in the evening, then have a drink in one of the outdoor cafés, from where you can appreciate the lit piazza and basilica.

One of the most memorable sights of nighttime Rome is the 12th-century gold mosaics on the façade of Santa Maria in Trastevere, their floodlit glow casting a gentle light over the piazza below.

Early church Santa Maria in Trastevere is among the oldest officially sanctioned places of worship in Rome. It was reputedly founded in AD222, allegedly on the spot where a fountain of olive oil had sprung from the earth on the day of Christ's birth (symbolizing the coming of the grace of God). Much of the present church was built in the 12th century during the reign of Innocent II, a member of the Papareschi, a prominent Trastevere family. Inside, the main colonnade of the nave is composed of reused and ancient Roman columns. The portico, containing fragments of Roman reliefs and

Clockwise from far left: a fountain graces the piazza outside the church; mosaics adorn the upper apse;. nighttime in Piazza di Santa Maria in Trastevere; detail of the upper apse mosaics; the gold mosaics on the façade; twenty-two columns from ancient monuments divide the nave from the aisles

inscriptions and medieval remains, was added in 1702 by Carlo Fontana, who was responsible for the fountain that graces the adjoining piazza.

Mosaics The façade mosaics probably date from the mid-12th century, and depict the Virgin and Child with 10 lamp-carrying companions. Long believed to portray the parable of the Wise and Foolish Virgins, their subject matter is contested, as several 'virgins' appear to be men and only two are carrying unlighted lamps (not the five of the parable). The mosaics of the upper apse inside the church, devoted to the glorification of the Virgin, date from the same period and are Byzantine-influenced works by Greek or Greek-trained craftsmen. Those below, depicting scenes from the life of the Virgin (1291), are by the mosaicist and fresco painter Pietro Cavallini.

THE BASICS

✚ E7

✉ Piazza Santa Maria in Trastevere

☎ 06 361 0836 or 06 581 4802

🕐 Daily 7.45–8/9 (may close 12.30–3.30 in winter)

🚌 H, 8, 780 Viale di Trastevere, 125 to Via Manara or 23, 280 to Lungotevere Raffaello Sanzio

♿ Wheelchair accessible

✋ Free

Villa Farnesina

TOP 25

The Salone delle Prospettive (left); Villa Farnesina's gardens, ideal for a walk (right)

THE BASICS

www.francopanini.it

🔲 E6

✉ Via della Lungara 230

☎ 06 6802 7268

🕐 Mon–Sat 9–1

🚌 23, 125, 280 to Lungotevere della Farnesina

♿ Moderate

HIGHLIGHTS

● Peruzzi's vibrant frescos of trompe l'oeil views of Rome in the Salone delle Prospetctive
● Peruzzi's *trompe l'oeil* views of Rome
● The gardens
● Raphael's *Trionfo di Galatea* (Triumph of Galatea)

TIP

● Within the building is also the National Print Collection (Gabinetto Nazionale delle Stampe), part of the National Institute of Graphics, which can be visited by permission

This is one of the most intimate and charming of all Rome's grand houses, known as much for its peaceful gardens as for its beautifully decorated interior, which contains works commissioned from Raphael and other artists by the villa's original owner, Agostino Chigi.

All to impress In 1508, Agostino Chigi, a wealthy banker from Siena, commissioned Baldasssare Puruzzi to build him a suburban villa. Here, Chigi entertained artists, princes and cardinals. His banquets were memorable: After the meal, Chigi would have the gold and silver dishes thrown into the Tiber to impress his guests with his wealth. What they did not know was that the plates were caught by safety nets and returned to the kitchens. In 1580, the villa was bought by the Farnese family, and it has been known as Villa Farnesina ever since.

Lots to admire On the ground floor are the Loggia of Galatea, with a much admired fresco by Raphael of the *Triumph of Galatea*, and the Loggia of Cupid and Psyche, frescoed to Raphael's designs by some of his pupils (including the future star of Mannerist painting, Giulio Romano). On the upper floor is the beautiful Salone delle Prospettive, with a fresco by Baldassare Peruzzi of a *trompe l'oeil* colonnade through which can be seen rural landscapes, villages and a town. Finally, visit Chigi's former bed chamber, decorated with an erotic fresco, *The Wedding Night of Alexander the Great and Roxane*, by Il Sodoma.

TOP 25

TRASTEVERE AND THE SOUTH

More to See

AVENTINO HILL

The most southernly of Rome's seven hills and one of the most beautiful quarters. Here the traffic and chaos of the city are left far behind, replaced by peaceful churches, charming cloisters, beautiful gardens and panoramic views over Trastevere and St. Peter's.

➕ G8 🚇 Circo Massimo 🚌 C3, 81, 160, 628, 715 to Via del Circo Massimo

GHETTO

This picturesque place, its narrow streets full of Jewish restaurants, pastry shops and workshops, is still a meeting place for the Roman-Jewish community. The 1904 synagogue, overlooking the Tiber, houses the Jewish Museum, its dome visible from all over the city.

➕ F6 **Museo:** ✉ Lungotevere Cenci ☎ 06 6840 0661 🕐 Mid-Jun–end Sep Sun–Thu 10–6.15, Fri 10–3.15 (closes earlier in winter) 🚌 23, 63, 280, 630, 780 ✋ Moderate

GIANICOLO

Not one of Rome's original seven hills, but the best view of Rome has to be from the Janiculum Hill. There are spectacular views all the way up from the Passeggiata del Gianicolo, a fine avenue that runs around the hill. En route visit the little Tempietto designed by Bramante in 1508, and the church of San Pietro in Montorio.

➕ D7 ✉ Passeggiata del Gianicolo 🕐 Tempietto Tue–Sun 9.30–12.30, 4–6 (2–4 Nov–end Apr); church daily 9–12, 4–6 🚌 44, 75, 115, 125 to the Gianicolo or Via Garibaldi

ISOLA TIBERINA

This small island in the Tiber with its medieval buildings and Roman bridges, feels like a safe haven, protected from the chaos of the city. The island is on a volcanic rock and its shape resembles that of a ship. Two bridges join the Isola Tiberina to the riverbanks: the Ponte Cestio dates back to the first century BC, and leads to Trastevere; while the Ponte Fabricio, built in 62BC, the only Roman bridge to survive intact, joins the island to the Ghetto.

➕ F7 🚌 H, 23, 63, 280, 780 to Lungotevere dei Cenci and all services to Via Arenula and Largo di Torre Argentina

From Gianicolo a panorama of Rome opens up before you

The narrow streets of the Ghetto quarter

ORTO BOTANICO

Trastevere has few open spaces, so these university gardens and their 8,000 or so botanical species provide a welcome oasis of green shade.

🔆 D7 ✉ Largo Cristina di Svezia 24, off Via Corsini ☎ 06 4991 7107 🕐 Tue–Sat 9.30–6.30 (5.30 in winter); closed holidays and Aug 🚌 23, 280 to Lungotevere Farnesina 🚻 Moderate

PALAZZO CORSINI

Though in a separate building, this gallery is part of the Palazzo Barberini's Galleria Nazionale. Originally part of the Corsini family's 17th-century collection, it became state property in 1883. Pictures from the 16th to 18th century hang alongside bronzes and sculptures in a series of elegant rooms.

🔆 E6 ✉ Via della Lungara 10 ☎ 06 6880 2323, reservations 06 328 101; www.ticketeria.it 🕐 Tue–Sun 8.30am–1.30pm 🚌 23, 280, 870 to Lungotevere Farnesina 🚻 Moderate

SANTA CECILIA IN TRASTEVERE

Enter the church through a delightful courtyard, with a portico supported by old granite columns and a lily garden with a central fountain. Next you pass a façade designed by Ferdinando Fuga in 1741. Crypt excavations and splendid 9th-century apse mosiacs depicting Jesus with saints Paul, Agata, Peter, Paschal, Valeriano and Cecilia are among Santa Cecilia's treasures. Another is the beautiful fresco *Last Judgement* (1293) by Pietro Cavallini, the remains of a medieval masterpiece that once covered the walls of the central nave but was mostly lost in an 18th-century restoration of the church. The fresco was moved to the nuns' choir where it can be viewed.

🔆 F8 ✉ Piazza di Santa Cecilia 22 ☎ 06 589 9289 or 06 581 2140 🕐 Daily 9.30–12.30, 4–6.30. Cavallini fresco Mon–Sat 10.15–12.15, Sun 11–12.30 🚌 23, 44, 125, 280, 780 to Viale Trastevere or Lungotevere Ripa 🚻 Church free; Cavallini fresco inexpensive; crypt expensive

SANTA MARIA IN COSMEDIN

This lovely old medieval church is best known for the Bocca della Verità, a

A charming courtyard fronts Santa Cecilia in Trastevere

Framed by overhanging branches, the ancient bridge linking Isola Tiberina with Trastevere

weather-beaten stone face (of the sea god Oceanus) once used by the ancient Romans as a drain cover. Inside, the church has a beautiful floor, twin pulpits, a bishop's throne and a stone choir screen, all done in fine Cosmati stone inlay. Most date from the 12th century, a little earlier than the impressive *baldacchino* (altar canopy), which was built by Deodato di Cosma in 1294. In a room off the right aisle is a mosaic depicting the *Adoration of the Magi*, almost all that remains of an 8th-century Greek church on the site.

➕ G7 ✉ Piazza della Bocca della Verità 18 ☎ 06 678 1419 ◷ Daily 9–1, 2–7 (6 in winter) 🚌 30, 44, 81, 95, 170 and other routes to Piazza Bocca della Verità or Lungotevere Pierleoni ♿ Free

SANTA SABINA

The lovely basilica of Santa Sabina, on the Aventine Hill, has kept its original 5th-century early Christian plan almost intact. Next to the church is a beautiful medieval cloister where St. Dominic is said to have planted the first orange tree in Rome, the descendants of

which still perfume the monk's garden. At the entrance, behind a front portico, is one of the church's main treasures. The entrance doors are divided into wooden panels, many of them survivors from the 5th-century church, carved with scenes from the Old and New Testaments.

➕ G8 ✉ Piazza Pietro d'Illiria 1 ☎ 06 574 3573 ◷ Daily 7–12.30, 3.30–7 (until 5.30 in winter) 🚇 Circo Massimo 🚌 C3, 81, 160, 628, 715 to Via del Circo Massimo ♿ Free

TEMPLES

The Tempio di Vesta and Tempio della Fortuna Virilis are the two best-preserved ancient temples in Rome—all but one of the 20 columns of the former remain standing. Both date from the 2nd century BC, the first named after its resemblance to a similar temple in the Roman Forum. The origins of the second, and the god to whom it was dedicated, remain a mystery.

➕ G7 ✉ 7 Piazza Bocca della Verità 🚌 C3, H, 81, 160, 175 and other services to Via del Teatro del Marcello and Piazza Bocca della Verità

Inside Santa Sabina, Rome's finest surviving 5th-century Basilica

The Bocca della Verita or 'Mouth of Truth', Santa Maria in Cosmedin

Ghetto to Trastevere

Discover two of Rome's less explored areas, the Ghetto and the Isola Tiberina, before crossing the Tiber to colourful Trastevere.

DISTANCE: 3.5km (2 miles)   **ALLOW:** 2–3hours

START

PIAZZA DEL CAMPIDOGLIO
➕ G6 🚌 C3, 40, 63, 70 and all other services to Piazza Venezia

1 Walk west down the ramp from Piazza del Campidoglio. Cross the road and go down Via d'Aracoeli. Take the second left alley just after the fountain directly into Piazza Margana.

2 Cross the piazza into Via dei Delfini and follow the street as it curves right into Via dei Funari. Walk along Via dei Funari to Piazza Mattei, home to the Fontana delle Tartarughe (▷ 51).

3 Continue past the fountain on Via dei Falegnami to busy Via Arenula. Turn left and then immediately left again on Via Santa Maria di Pianto.

4 Continue along Via Santa Maria di Pianto as it becomes Via del Portico d'Ottavia, named after the gateway on the left. Follow the road as it bears right.

END

PIAZZA DI SANTA MARIA IN TRASTEVER▮
➕ E7 🚌 H, 8, 170 to Viale Trastevere or 125 to Vi▮ della Sca▮

8 In Piazza Sidney Sonnino go left down Via della Lungaretta to Piazza di Santa Maria in Trastevere. Some of the prettiest streets are north of here.

7 Continue to the church of Santa Cecilia (▷ 68) on your right. With your back to the church, turn left and then first left down Via del Genovesi. Continue straight as this street becomes Via G. C. Santini and turn right at Viale Trastevere.

6 Go over the Lungotevere and cross the Ponte Fabricio to the Isola Tiberina (▷ 67). Leave the island on the Ponte Cestio and cross over the Lungotevere. Go left and bear right through Piazza Piazza dei Ponziani and right on Via dei Vascellari.

5 Note the Teatro di Marcello to your left and Rome's main synagogue on your right.

Shopping

ALMOST CORNER BOOKSHOP

Tiny bookshop stocking an interesting and unusual selection of English language books, especially considering its small size. The prices are competitive and it is particularly good on biography and history, with a strong emphasis on Rome and Italy. Helpful and knowledgeable staff.

⊞ E7 ⊠ Via del Moro 45 ☎ 06 583 6942 ◑ Mon–Sat 10–1.30, 3.30–8, Sun 11–1.30, 3.30–8; closed Sun in Aug

CASIMON

This glorious shop sells a variety of objects in marble, stone, glass and semi-precious stones, from ornamental marble balls and bookends to tables and lampshades.

⊞ F7 ⊠ Via della Lungaretta 90 ☎ 06 581 4860 ◑ Daily 11am–midnight

DROGHERIA INNOCENZI

Set on bustling Piazza San Cosimato, this foodie's haven is stacked high with sacks of pasta and polenta, regional specialties and products from abroad that are difficult to find elsewhere. Such is the fame of this shop, people travel from far and wide to stock up, aided by the friendly and attentive staff.

⊞ E8 ⊠ Piazza San Cosimato 66 ☎ 06 581 2725 ◑ Daily 8.30–1.30, 4.30–8; closed Thu pm

LUMIÈRES

Unassuming shop crammed with goods. If an interesting lamp from the French art deco or Italian Liberty periods is what you're after, this is the place to come. Choose from dozens of antique lamps, all fully restored. Or bring your own lamp to be restored by an artisan.

⊞ E7 ⊠ Vicolo del Cinque 48 ☎ 06 580 3614 ◑ Mon– Sat 10–1, 4–8.30, Sun 4–8

PANDORA

This is an unusual but

LOCAL SHOPPING

Roman supermarkets are few and far between and most food is still bought in tiny local shops known as *alimentari*. Every street of every 'village' or district in the city has one or more of these general shops, a source of everything from olive oil and pasta to candles and corn and bunion treatments. They are also good places to buy picnic provisions—many sell bread and wine—and most have a delicatessen counter that will make you a sandwich (*panino*) from the meats and cheeses on display. For something a little more special, or for food gifts to take home, visit Via della Croce, a street renowned for its wonderful delicatessens.

tasteful store, with a great selection of contemporary Venetian glass items, Italian handmade ceramics, ethnic and handmade jewellery, small antique pieces, and accessories such as scarves and bags.

⊞ E7 ⊠ Piazza Santa Maria in Trastevere 6 ☎ 06 581 7145 ◑ Daily 10–10

PIAZZA SAN COSIMATO

It is a great shame that very few visitors manage to discover what this excellent mid-size general food market in Trastevere has to offer.

⊞ E8 ⊠ Piazza San Cosimato ◑ Mon–Sat 7am–1pm

PORTA PORTESE

Everything and anything is for sale at this famous flea market, though the few genuine antiques are highly priced. By midmorning crowds are huge, so come early and guard your belongings.

⊞ F8 ⊠ Via Porta Portese-Via Ippolito Nuevo ◑ Sun 6.30am–2pm

VOLPETTI

This Aladdin's cave of delights has been established for more than 100 years and is justly famous. Handmade pasta, whole hams, cheeses, pungent truffle and extra virgin olive oils are just some of the delights.

⊞ G9 ⊠ Via Marmorata 47 ☎ 06 574 2352 ◑ Mon–Sat 8–2, 5–8.15

Entertainment and Nightlife

AKAB-CAVE
www.akabcave.com
In the lively Testaccio area, this very popular and long-established club is on two levels (one underground—hence Cave) with a garden area and varied music policy. International DJs and live rock bands.
✚ Off map at G9 ✉ Via di Monte Testaccio 68–69 ☎ 06 5725 0585 🕔 Tue–Sat 11pm–4.30am 🚇 Piramide 🚌 23, 44, 170, 280 to Piazza di Porta San Paolo or Via Monte Testaccio 💲 Expensive

L'ALIBI
Primarily a gay disco, but not exclusively, L'Alibi is one of the most reliable (and most established) clubs now mushrooming in trendy Testaccio.
✚ Off map at G9 ✉ Via di Monte Testaccio 40–44 ☎ 06 574 3448 🕔 Wed–Sun midnight–5am 🚇 Piramide 🚌 23, 44, 170, 280 to Piazza di Porta San Paolo or Via Monte Testaccio 💲 Expensive

BAR SAN CALISTO
Bohemian and vibrant—this is where the locals hang out. The piazza-side tables give a window on the real Trastevere and cheap prices make it a great spot to linger. Chocolate, hot with cream in winter and cooling as a 'gelato' in summer, is among Rome's best.
✚ E7 ✉ Piazza San Calisto ☎ 06 583 5869 🕔 Mon–Sat 5.30am–2am 🚌 H, 8, 780 to Viale Trastevere

BIG MAMA
www.bigmama.it
Rome's best blues club; also hosts rock and jazz.
✚ F8 ✉ Vicolo San Francesco a Ripa 18 ☎ 06 581 2551 🕔 Mid-Sep–end Jun Tue–Sat 9pm–1.30am 🚌 H, 8, 780 to Viale di Trastevere 🎫 Membership (moderate)

CAFFÈ LATINO
Testaccio oldest club, devoted to eating, drinking, live music and dance sessions. Mostly jazz, but rap, blues and other genres.
✚ Off map at G9 ✉ Via Monte Testaccio 96 ☎ 06 5728 8556 🕔 Sep–end Jul, Tue–Thu, Sun 10.30pm–2.30am, Fri, Sat 10.30pm–4.30am 🚇 Piramide 🚌 3, 23, 30, 75, 280, 716 to Via Marmorata 🎫 Membership (expensive)

ENOTECA TRASTEVERE
Tavernlike wine bar with

more than 900 wines. On weekends, a pianist plays jazz and swing. There are tables outside in summer.
✚ F7 ✉ Via della Lungaretta 86 ☎ 06 588 5659 🕔 Daily 6pm–2am; closed Wed Dec–end Feb 🚌 H, 175 to Piazza Sidney Sonnino

LETTERE CAFFÈ GALLERY
The perfect spot for books, blues, booze and jazz in this literary café where the bar buzzes after 10pm with music.
✚ F8 ✉ Via San Francesco a Ripa 100-101 ☎ 06 6456 1916. 🕔 Daily 5pm–2am (closed Aug) 🚌 23, 115, 125 or tram 8 to Piazza Trilussa

NUOVO SACHER
www.sacherfilm.eu
Although dedicated to Italian film talent, this cinema shows foreign films in *versione originale* on Monday. Seats up to 360 people; in summer there are screenings outside in the courtyard.
✚ F8 ✉ Largo Ascianghi 1 ☎ 06 581 8116 🕔 Daily 6–9.30 🚌 H, 8, 780 to Viale di Trastevere 💲 Moderate

TEATRO VASCELLO
On the edge of Trastevere, this is a small but good venue for experimental dance and some classic ballet, and multimedia events.
✚ D8 ✉ Via Giacinto Carini 72 ☎ 06 588 1021 🕔 Sep–end Jun, Tue–Sat 5.30–9, Sun 3–5 🚌 44, 75, 115, 710, 870

Restaurants

PRICES

Prices are approximate, based on a 3-course meal for one person.

€€€   over €50
€€   €30–€50
€   under €30

ALBERTO CIARLA (€€€)

This is among Rome's best fish restaurants, with a fine wine list. The food is elegantly presented, the candlelight lovely and the service impeccable.
E8 ✉ Piazza San Cosimato 40 ☎ 06 581 6068 or 06 581 6068 ⏰ Dinner only Mon–Sat; closed 2 weeks in Aug and 1 week Jan 🚊 H, 8, 630, 780 to Viale di Trastevere

ALBERTO PICA (€)

Around 20 varieties of excellent quality ice cream; try their specialties like green apple (*mele verde*) and Sicilian citrus (*agrumi di Sicilia*).
F6 ✉ Via della Seggiola 12, Cenci ☎ 06 686 8405 ⏰ Mon–Sat 8am–1.30am (also Sun 4pm–2am Apr–end Oct); closed 2 weeks in Aug 🚊 8 to Via Arenula and 8, 46, 62, 63, 64, 70, 87, 186, 492 to Largo di Torre Argentina

AUGUSTO (€)

One of Trastevere's last remaining inexpensive and authentic family-run *trattorie*, with 50 places. No credit cards.
E7 ✉ 10 ✉ Piazza de' Renzi 15 ☎ 06 580 3798

⏰ Daily 12–3.30, 8–11; closed Aug 🚊 23, 280 to Lungotevere Sanzio or H, 8, 780 to Piazza Sidney Sonnino

BIBLI (€€)

www.bibli.it
This Trastevere bookshop-cum-cafeteria is particularly popular for Sunday brunch. A selection of pastas, quiches, coucous with vegetable dishes are served buffet style.
F7 ✉ Via dei Fienaroli 28 ☎ 06 588 4097 ⏰ Daily 11am–midnight; Mon 5.30–11.30 buffet-style dinner 🚊 H, 23, 44, 56, 75, 280 to Viale Trastevere or Piazza Sonnino

CHECCHINO DAL 1887 (€€€)

www.checchino-dal-1887.com
Robust appetites are required for the menu at this Testaccio establishment. Quintessential Roman dishes relying largely on offal are the

BUYING ICE CREAM

Ice cream (*gelato*) in a proper *gelateria* is sold either in a cone (*un cono*) or a paper cup (*una coppa*). Specify which you want and then decide how much you wish to pay: sizes of cone and cup go up in price bands, usually starting small and ending enormous. You can select up to two or three varieties (more in bigger tubs) and will usually be asked if you want a swirl of cream (*panna*) to round things off.

specialty. Reservations are advisable.
Off map G9 ✉ Via Monte Testaccio 30 ☎ 06 574 6318 ⏰ Tue–Sat 12.30–3, 8–11; closed Aug, 24 Dec–2 Jan 🚊 3, 60, 75, 118 to Piramide

CHECCO ER CARETTIERE (€€–€€€)

A Trastevere beacon to traditional cooking surveyed by black and white photos of celebrities. Good seafood and homemade specialties feature. Outside patio and internal garden room for smokers.
E7 ✉ Via Benedetta,10 ☎ 06 580 0985 ⏰ Wed–Mon 12.30–3, 7.30–midnight 🚊 23, 115, 125 or tram 8 to Piazza Trilussa

DA FELICE (€€)

This Testaccio institution has been smartened up since the retirement of Felice, but he's still on hand to make sure that the *trattoria* fare is as good as ever.
Off map G9 ✉ Via Mastro Giorgio, 29, Testaccio ☎ 06 574 6800 ⏰ Mon–Sat 12.30–3, 8–11.30, Sun 12.30–3; closed 3 weeks in Aug 🚊 Tram to Via Marmorata

DAR POETA (€)

A very popular and long-established little pizzeria hidden in a quiet street. The interior is simple but the pizza (and puddings) are excellent.
E7 ✉ Vicolo di Bologna 45 ☎ 06 588 0516 ⏰ Daily dinner only 7.30–11 🚊 8, 870 and all services to Trastevere

TRASTEVERE AND THE SOUTH

RESTAURANTS

DA VITTORIO (€)

Tiny Neapolitan-run Trastevere pizzeria that makes a good standby if Ivo (▷ 74) is busy.

🕂 E7 ✉ Via di San Cosimato 14a, off Piazza San Calisto ☎ 06 580 0353 🕐 Mon–Sat 7.30pm–midnight 🚌 H, 8, 780 to Viale di Trastevere

FRENI E FRIZIONI (€)

This shabby bar is ultra cool and attracts gilded young Romans who spill out onto the small raised square. Come here for *aperitivi*. (▷ 57, panel).

🕂 E7 ✉ Via del Politeama 4-6 ☎ 06 5833 4210 🕐 Daily 10am–2am 🚌 H, 8, 780 to Viale di Trastevere

GIGGETTO (€)

A famous Romano-Jewish restaurant in the Ghetto district; almost as good and cheaper than Piperno (▷ 74).

🕂 G6 ✉ Via Portico d'Ottavia 21a ☎ 06 686 1105 🕐 Tue–Sun 12.30–2.30, 7.30–10.30 🚌 H, 8, 63 to Via Arenula and 46, 62, 63, 70 and other services to Largo di Torre Argentina

IVO (€)

The best-known of Trastevere's pizzerias. Lines are common but turnover is quick.

🕂 E7 ✉ Via di San Francesco a Ripa 158 ☎ 06 581 7082 🕐 Wed–Mon 5.30pm–2am; closed 3 weeks Aug 🚌 H, 8, 780 to Viale di Trastevere

PANATTONI (€)

Big, bright and often busy, Panattoni is known locally as 'L'Obitorio' (The Morgue) on account of its characteristic cold marble-topped tables. Watch the chef flip the pizzas at the oven. Arrive early to get a table outside.

🕂 F8 ✉ Viale di Trastevere 53 ☎ 06 580 0919 🕐 Thu–Tue 7pm–2am; closed 3 weeks Aug 🚌 H, 8, 780 to Viale di Trastevere

PARIS (€€)

An extremely popular and elegant little restaurant known for its fish, pastas and Roman cuisine. Outside tables for alfresco dining. Reserve ahead.

🕂 E7 ✉ Piazza San Callisto 7a ☎ 06 581 5378 🕐 Tue–Sat 12.30–3, 8–11, Sun 12.30–3; closed 3 weeks in Aug 🚌 H, 8, 780 to Piazza

---

BAR ETIQUETTE

You almost always pay a premium to sit down (inside or outside) and to enjoy the privilege of waiter service in Roman bars. If you stand—which is less expensive—the procedure is to pay for what you want first at the cash desk (*la cassa*). You then take your receipt (*lo scontrino*) to the bar and repeat your order (a tip slapped down on the bar will work wonders in attracting the bar person's attention). Pastry shops, cafés and ice-cream shops often double as excellent all-around bars to be enjoyed during the day.

Sidney Sonnino or 23, 280 to Lungotevere Sanzio

PIPERNO (€€)

Much Roman cuisine is based on the city's Jewish culinary traditions. The famous and resolutely traditional Piperno has been a temple to Romano-Jewish cuisine for over a century. Reserve ahead.

🕂 F6 ✉ Via Monte de' Cenci 9 ☎ 06 6880 6629/ 2772 🕐 Tue–Sat 12.15–2.30, 8–10.30, Sun 12.15–3; closed Aug 🚌 H, 8, 63 to Via Arenula and 8, 46, 62, 63, 64, 70, 87, 492 to Largo di Torre Argentina

SORA LELLA (€€–€€€)

Founded by the actress Sora Lella, and now presided over by her son and nephews, this is a two-room, wood-panel former *trattoria* on the Isola Tiberina. Roman cooking, with menu and daily specials.

🕂 G7 ✉ Via Ponte Quattro Capi 16 ☎ 06 686 1601 🕐 Mon–Sat 12.30–2.30, 7.30–10.30; closed 15–20 Aug 🚌 23, 23, 63, 280 to Lungotevere dei Cenci or Lungotevere degli Anguillara

VOLPETTI PIÙ (€)

A splendid *tavola calda* serving hot food such as soups, meats, pasta and pizza. The price is excellent value and the quality is exemplary.

🕂 Off map G9 ✉ Via A Volta, 8 Testaccio ☎ 06 574 4306 🕐 Mon–Sat 10.30–3.30, 5.30–9.30 🚌 Tram to Via Marmorata.

Northern Rome is a wonderful medley of open spaces, notably the Villa Borghese, historical and cultural attractions such as the Fontana di Trevi and the Spanish Steps, and Rome's finest shopping streets.

Fontana di Trevi

Remember to toss a coin in the fountain (left); the Trevi in all its floodlit glory (right)

THE BASICS

+ G5
- Piazza Fontana di Trevi
- Always open
- Spagna or Barberini
- C3, 52, 53, 61, 62, 71, 95, 117, 119 and other routes to Via del Corso and Via del Tritone
- Access via cobbled street
- Free

HIGHLIGHTS

- *Oceanus* (Neptune)
- *Allegory of Health* (right of *Oceanus*)
- *Virgin Indicating the Spring to Soldiers*
- *Allegory of Abundance* (left of *Oceanus*)
- *Agrippa Approving the Design of the Aqueduct*
- *Triton with Horse* (on the right, symbolizing the ocean in repose)
- *Triton with Horse* (on the left, symbolizing a tempestuous sea)
- *Façade of Santi Vincenzo e Anastasio*
- *Baroque interior of Santa Maria in Trivio*

There is no lovelier surprise than that which confronts you as you emerge from the tight warren of streets around the Fontana di Trevi, the city's most famous fountain—a sight 'silvery to the eye and ear', in the words of Charles Dickens.

Virgin discovery In its earliest guise the Fontana di Trevi lay at the end of the Aqua Virgo, or Acqua Vergine, an aqueduct built by Agrippa in 19BC (supposedly filled with Rome's sweetest waters). The spring that fed it was reputedly discovered by a virgin, hence its name. (She is said to have shown her discovery to some Roman soldiers, a scene—along with Agrippa's approval of the aqueduct's plans—described in bas-reliefs on the fountain's second tier.) The fountain's liveliness and charm is embodied in the pose of *Oceanus*, the central figure, and the two giant tritons and their horses (symbolizing a calm and a stormy sea) drawing his chariot. Other statues represent Abundance and Health and, above, the Four Seasons, which each carry gifts.

The fountains A new fountain was built in 1453, ordered by Pope Nicholas V who paid for it by taxing wine. Its name came from the three roads (*tre vie*) that converged on the piazza. The present fountain was commissioned by Pope Clement XII in 1732 and finished in 1762: Its design was inspired by the Arch of Constantine and is attributed to Nicola Salvi, with possible contributions from Bernini. Those wishing to return to Rome toss a coin (over the shoulder) into the fountain.

Canova's Paolina
Borghese *(left) and*
Bernini's *Rape of*
Proserpine *(right)*

TOP 25

Museo e Galleria Borghese

The Galleria Borghese may be small, but what it lacks in quantity it makes up for in quality. It combines paintings and sculptures, including many masterpieces by Gian Lorenzo Bernini, Raphael, Caravaggio and others.

Seductress The Villa Borghese was designed in 1613 as a summer retreat for Cardinal Scipione Borghese, nephew of Pope Paul V, who accumulated most of the collection (acquired by the state in 1902). Scipione was an enthusiastic patron of Bernini, whose works dominate the gallery. His *David* (1623–24) is said to be a self-portrait, while *Apollo and Daphne* (1622–25), in the next room, is considered his masterpiece. Other Bernini works include the *Rape of Proserpine* (1622) and *Truth Unveiled by Time* (1652).

The setting The museum is set in the splendid grounds of the Villa Borghese, (▷ 87), to the north of the city, and is now Rome's largest public park—200 acres (80ha) with a total of five museums, gardens, lakes fountains and a deer park. Before Cardinal Scipone made the grounds the base of his 17th-century pleasure palace, they were vineyards.

The paintings Foremost in this wonderful collection are works by Raphael (*The Deposition of Christ*, 1507), Titian (*Sacred and Profane Love*, 1512), Caravaggio (*Boy with a Fruit Basket* and *Madonna dei Palafrenieri*, 1605) and Correggio (*Danae*, 1530).

THE BASICS

www.galleriaborghese.it
⊞ J2
✉ Piazzale Scipione Borghese 5
☎ 06 841 7645; obligatory reservations 06 328 101; www.ticketeria.it
🕐 Tue–Sun 9–7; closed public holidays
Ⓢ Spagna or Flaminio
🚌 116 to Viale del Museo Borghese, or 52, 53, 910 to Via Pinciana or C3, 19 to Via delle Belle Arti
♿ Steps to front entrance
💲 Expensive

HIGHLIGHTS

● Antonio Canova's sculpture of Paolina Borghese (1804), who was Napoleon's sister and wife of Camillo Borghese. She was shown bare-breasted and looked every bit as seductive as she was in real-life

Palazzo Barberini

Frescos outlined in gold adorn the palazzo (left); Raphael's La Fornarina (right)

THE BASICS

🔲 J4
✉ Via delle Quattro Fontane 13
☎ 06 32810; online booking www.ticketeria.it
🕐 Tue–Sun 8.30–7.30
Ⓜ Barberini
🚌 52, 53, 61, 62, 63, 71, 80, 95, 116, 119 to Via del Tritone or H, 40, 60, 64, 70, 71, 116T, 170 to Via Nazionale
♿ Few
🎫 Moderate

HIGHLIGHTS

● Elicoidale
● *Madonna and Child* and *Annunciation*, Filippo Lippi
● *Holy Family* and *Madonna and Saints*, Andrea del Sarto
● *Madonna and Child*, Beccafumi
● Borromini's false-perspective window on the top floor
● *Adoration of the Shepherds* and *Baptism of Christ*, El Greco
● *Judith and Holofernes* and *Narciso*, Caravaggio
● *Beatrice Cenci*, attributed to Guido Reni
● *Henry VIII*, attributed to Holbein
● *The Triumph of Divine Providence*, Pietro da Cortona (Gran Salone)

The magnificent Palazzo Barberini—designed by Bernini, Borromini and Carlo Maderno—houses a stupendous ceiling fresco and one of Rome's finest art collections, the Galleria Nazionale d'Arte Antica.

Urban's grandeur The palace was commissioned by Maffeo Barberini for his family when he became Pope Urban VIII in 1623. It was begun by Carlo Maderno and completed by Bernini. The epitome of Rome's high baroque style, it is a maze of suites, apartments and staircases, many still swathed in their sumptuous original decoration. Overshadowing all is the Gran Salone, dominated by Pietro da Cortona's rich ceiling frescos, glorifying Urban as an agent of Divine Providence. The central windows and oval spiral staircase (Scala Elicoidale) are the work of Borromini.

The collection *'Antica'* here means old rather than ancient. Probably the most popular painting in the collection is Raphael's *La Fornarina* (also attributed to Giulio Romano). It is reputedly a portrait of one of the artist's several mistresses, identified later as the daughter of a *fornaio* (baker). It was executed in the year of the painter's death, a demise brought on, it is said, by his mistress's unrelenting passion. Elsewhere, eminent Italian works from Filippo Lippi, Andrea del Sarto, Caravaggio and Guido Reni stand alongside paintings by leading foreign artists. Also here is a rich collection of paintings, furniture, ceramics and other beautiful decorative arts.

This popular meeting place (left and right) is used as a stage for fashion shows (middle)

Neither old nor particularly striking, the Spanish Steps are nonetheless one of Rome's most popular meeting points, thanks largely to their views, at the heart of Piazza di Spagna in the city's exclusive shopping district.

Spanish Steps Despite their name, the Spanish Steps were commissioned by the French ambassador, Étienne Gueffier, who in 1723 sought to link Piazza di Spagna with the French-owned church of Trinità dei Monti on the hill above. A century earlier the piazza had housed the headquarters of the Spanish ambassador to the Holy See, hence the name of the steps and the square.

Around the steps At the base of the steps is the Fontana della Barcaccia, commissioned in 1627 by Urban VIII and designed either by Gian Lorenzo Bernini or by his less famous father, Pietro. The eccentric design represents a half-sunken boat. As you face the steps from below, to your right stands the Museo Keats–Shelley, a fascinating collection of literary memorabilia and a working library housed in the lodgings where the poet John Keats died in 1821. At the top of the steps you can enjoy views past Palazzo Barberini (▷ 80) and toward the Quirinal Hill; walk into the simple Trinità dei Monti, with its outside double stairs by Domenico Fontana; and visit the beautiful gardens of the 16th-century Villa Medici, the seat of the French Academy in Rome, where scholars study painting, sculpture, architecture, engraving and music.

THE BASICS

➕ G4
✉ Piazza di Spagna
☎ Villa Medici 06 679 8381
🕐 Spanish Steps always open. Trinità dei Monti daily 10–12.30, 4–6. Villa Medici occasionally open for exhibitions
🍴 Babington's Tea Rooms
🚇 Spagna
🚌 119 to Piazza di Spagna
♿ None for the Spanish Steps
💶 Free

HIGHLIGHTS

● Spanish Steps
● Museo Keats–Shelley (▷ 87)
● Trinità dei Monti
● Fontana della Barcaccia
● Babington's Tea Rooms
● Villa Medici gardens
● Pincio Gardens (▷ 87)

Palazzo Massimo
alle Terme

HIGHLIGHTS

● *Niobid from the Hortus Sallustiani* (Room VIII)
● The collection of coins in the basement
● *The Sleeping Hermaphrodite* (Room VII)
● House of Livia (Room II)
● The Villa Farnesina (Gallery II, Rooms III–V)

TIP

● The combined ticket is valid for all parts of the Museo Nazionale Romano, notably the Palazzo Altemps.

A sublime collection of Greek and Roman sculpture with outstanding and unique displays of ancient Roman wall paintings and mosaics dating from end of the Republican age to the late Imperial age.

The building The Palazzo Massimo is an elegant and airy 19th-century palace, beautifully renovated for the millennium. The palace, designed by Camillo Pistrucci, was built in the late 19th century by the Massimo family to replace an earlier one demolished to make way for the Termini station. In 1981 the palace was acquired by the state, and in the 1990s it was transformed into one of Rome's most attractive museums. The palace has four floors of museum space, a modern library, a conference room and a computer-based documentation area.

Lovingly restored, the Palazzo Massimo was a Jesuit college until 1960 (left) but now houses outstanding displays of ancient Roman wall paintings and mosaics (right)

The collection One of the two buildings (the other being Palazzo Altemps, ▷ 42–43) housing Rome's magnificent Classical collections. Here you'll find some of Rome's greatest treasures, ranging from naked gods and games players to sarcophagi and goddesses. Don't miss the superb portrait busts or the wonderful Roman frescos and mosaics on the upper floor.

Lancellotti Discobolus This fine marble copy of the great *Discus Thrower* dates from the mid-second century AD, and is one of the most famous copies of the 5th-century BC works. Discovered in the 18th century, it was sent to Germany during World War II and returned in 1948. It reproduces an original bronze, showing an athlete throwing a discus—probably the work of Myron, a Greek sculptor renowned for his portraits of athletes.

THE BASICS

✚ K5

✉ Piazza dei Cinquecento 67–Largo di Villa Peretti 1

☎ Reservations 06 3996 7700

🕐 Tue–Sun 9–7.45

🚇 Termini or Reppublicca

🚌 All services to Termini and Piazza dei Cinquecento

💷 Expensive (joint pass available with Palazzo Altemps, Crypta Balbi and Terme di Diocleziano)

Santa Maria del Popolo

Carracci's Assumption of the Virgin (left); inside is a wealth of artistic works (right)

THE BASICS

+ F2
✉ Piazza del Popolo 12
☎ 06 361 0836
🕐 Mon–Sat 7–12, 4–7, Sun 8–1, 4.30–7.30
Ⓜ Flaminio
🚌 117, 119 to Piazza del Popolo
♿ Few
💲 Free

HIGHLIGHTS

● Cappella Costa with the tombs of Giovanni Borgia, son of Pope Alexander VI (1492–1503) and his mother Vannozza Cattenei
● *Coronation of the Virgin*, Pinturicchio
● Tombs of Ascanio Sforza and Girolamo Basso della Rovere
● Fresco: *Life of San Girolamo*, Tiberio d'Assisi
● *Delphic Sybil*, Pinturicchio
● Altar, Andrea Bregno
● The oldest stained glass windows in Rome

Santa Maria del Popolo's appeal stems from its intimate size and location, and from a wonderfully varied and rich collection of works of art ranging from masterpieces by Caravaggio to some of Rome's earliest stained-glass windows.

Renaissance achievement Founded in 1099 on the site of Nero's grave, Santa Maria del Popolo was rebuilt by Pope Sixtus IV in 1472 and extended later by Bramante and Bernini. The right nave's first chapel, the Cappella della Rovere, is decorated with frescos—*Life of San Girolamo* (1485–90)—by Tiberio d'Assisi, a pupil of Pinturicchio whose *Nativity* (c1490) graces the chapel's main altar. The apse contains two fine stained-glass windows (1509) by the French artist Guillaume de Marcillat. On either side are the greatest of the church's monuments: the tombs of the cardinals Ascanio Sforza (1505, left) and Girolamo Basso della Rovere (1507, right). Both are the work of Andrea Sansovino. High on the walls are superb and elegant frescos (1508–10) of the Virgin, Evangelists, the Fathers of the Church and Sybils by Pinturicchio.

North nave The first chapel of the left transept, the Cappella Cerasi, contains three major paintings: the altarpiece, *Assumption of the Virgin*, by Annibale Carracci; and Caravaggio's dramatic *Conversion of St. Paul* and the *Crucifixion of St. Peter* (all 1601). The famous Cappella Chigi (1513), the second chapel in the north aisle, was commissioned by the Sienese banker Agostino Chigi.

Villa Giulia

Villa Giulia, built to a design by Giacomo da Vignola, displays beautiful frescos

The Museo Nazionale Etrusca di Villa Giulia houses the world's greatest collection of Etruscan art and objects. The exhibits are not always perfectly presented, but it is a revelation to dis-cover this mysterious civilization.

The villa Built in 1550–55 as a country house and garden for the hedonistic Pope Julius III, the Villa Giulia was designed by some of the leading architects of the day, including Michelangelo and Georgio Vasari.

The collection The exhibits are generally divided between finds from Etruscan sites in northern Etruria (western central Italy) and from excavations in the south (Nemi and Praeneste), including objects made by the Greeks. Most notable are the Castellani exhibits, which include vases, cups and ewers, and jewellery from the Minoan period (the latter collection is one of the villa's special treasures). To see the most striking works of art, be selective. Pick through the numerous vases noting the *Tomba del Guerriero* and the *Cratere a Volute*. Note also the *Sarcofago degli Sposi*, a 6th-century BC sarcophagus with figures of a married couple reclining together on a banqueting couch; the engraved marriage coffer known as the *Cista Ficoroni* (4th century BC); the giant terra-cotta figures, *Hercules and Apollo*; the temple sculptures from Falerii Veteres; and the valuable 7th-century BC relics in gold, silver, bronze and ivory from the Barberini and Bernardini tombs in Praeneste, 39km (24 miles) east of Rome.

THE BASICS

🔳 G1

✉ Piazzale di Villa Giulia 9

☎ 06 322 6571; reservations 06 824 620 online booking, www.ticketeria.it

🕐 Tue–Sat 8.30am–7.30pm, Sun and holidays 9–2

🍴 Café and shop

🚌 3 or 19 to Viale delle Belle Arti

♿ Good

💷 Moderate

HIGHLIGHTS

● *Lamine d'Oro*, Sala di Pyrgi: a gold tablet
● Villa's manneristic architectural style, preferred by Michelangelo
● Vase: *Cratere a Volute*
● Finds from Falerii Veteres
● The gruesome frieze displaying the Greek boxer (400BC) eating the brain of his opponent
● Marriage coffer: *Cista Ficoroni*
● Gardens with Nymphaeum and reconstructed 'Temple of Alatri'

More to See

FONTANA DEL TRITONE

Like its companion piece, the Fontana delle Api, the Fountain of Triton (1643) was also designed by Bernini for Urban VIII. One of the sculptor's earliest fountains, the Fontana del Tritone depicts four dolphins supporting twin scallop shells bearing the Barberini coat of arms, on which the triumphant Triton is enthroned.

✚ H4 ✉ Piazza Barberini 🚇 Barberini 🚌 52, 53, 61, 62, 80, 95, 116, 119 to Piazza Barberini or Via del Tritone

GALLERIA DELL'ACCADEMIA DI SAN LUCA

www.accademiasanluca.it

The gallery was founded to promote the training of artists in Renaissance techniques. From 1633, every artist member of the academy had to donate a work of art, resulting in a great collection that includes paintings by Raphael, Canova, Van Dyck, Rubens and Titian, to name a few.

✚ H4 ✉ Piazza dell'Accademia di San Luca 77 ☎ 06 679 8850 🕐 Mon–Fri 9–1, Mon, Thu also 3–6; closed Aug 🚇 Spagna or Barberini 🚌 52, 53, 60, 61, 62, 71, 80, 85, 160, 850 to Piazza San Silvestro 🖐 Free

MUSEO DELL'ARA PACIS

www.ara-pacis-museum.com

Augustus's Altar of Peace, now contained within architect Richard Meier's controversial glass pavilion (opened in 2006) is decorated with bas-reliefs from 9BC. It was built to celebrate Augustus's triumphal return to Rome after campaigns in Spain and Gaul, and to commemorate the peace he had established throughout the Roman world. The outside of the enclosure is decorated with mythological scenes and grand processional friezes in which life-size figures portray Augustus, the imperial family, officials and other notables. While the altar itself was rebuilt in the early 20th century, Meier's futuristic glass pavilion that houses it is the first architectural work built in the historic centre since the fall of fascism to the present 21st century.

✚ F4 ✉ Lungotevere in Augusta ☎ 06 8205 9127 🕐 Tue–Sun 9–7 🚇 Spagna 🚌 224, 913 to Piazza Augusto Imperatore or

Augustus's Altar of Peace, a memorial to the peace brought about by Augustus

A feature at the Galleria dell'Accademia di San Luca

224, 590, 628, 926 to Lungotevere in Augusta or 117, 119 to Via di Ripetta 🚇 Moderate

MUSEO KEATS–SHELLEY

www.keats-shelley-house.org

Since 1909 this has been a museum and library for students of the Romantic poets Keats and Shelley. Books, pictures and essays lie scattered around the 18th-century house.

🔒 G4 ✉ Piazza di Spagna ☎ 06 678 4235 🕐 Mon–Fri 9–1, 3–6, Sat 11–2, 3–6 🚇 Spagna 🚌 119 to Piazza di Spagna 🚇 Moderate

PINCIO

The park was laid out in the early 19th century. Walk to the Pincio from Piazza del Popolo or Piazza di Spagna to enjoy wonderful views (best at dusk) across the rooftops to St. Peter's.

🔒 G2 ✉ Piazza del Pincio 🕐 Daily dawn–dusk 🚌 95, 117, 119 to Piazzale Flaminio or Piazza del Popolo 🚇 Free

SANTA MARIA DELLA CONCEZIONE

Lying in the crypt of Santa Maria della Concezione, built in 1624, are the

remains of 4,000 Capuchin monks, some still dressed in jaunty clothes, the bones of others crafted into macabre chandeliers and bizarre wall decorations. The bodies were originally buried in soil especially imported from Jerusalem. When this ran out they were left uncovered, a practice that continued until 1870.

🔒 H4 ✉ Via Vittorio Veneto 27 ☎ 06 452 850 🕐 Church daily 7–12, 3.45–7. Crypt (Cimitero dei Cappuccini) daily 9–12, 4–6 🚌 52, 53, 80, 95, 116, 119 to Via Vittorio Veneto 🚇 Free (donation to visit crypt)

VILLA BORGHESE

Rome's largest central park (▷ 88) was laid out between 1613 and 1616 as the grounds of the Borghese family's summer villa. Redesigned in the 18th century, it still provides a shady retreat. Walkways, woods and lakes are complemented by fountains, a racetrack, zoo and playgrounds.

🔒 H2 ✉ Porta Pinciana-Via Flaminia 🕐 Daily dawn–dusk; Bioparco daily 9.30–5/6 🚇 Flaminio 🚌 3, 19, 88, 95, 116, 117, 119, 495 🚇 Free; Bioparco expensive

The crypt, Santa Maria della Concezione

The Temple of Esculapio, at the Villa Borghese

Villa Borghese

A stroll in this park, once the estate of Cardinal Scipione Borghese, is the perfect antidote to the turmoil of Rome's busy streets.

DISTANCE: 2km (1.2 miles) **ALLOW:** 2 hours

START

PIAZZA DEL POPOLO
✛ F2 🚌 117, 119

1 Piazza del Popolo is the site of two almost identical churches, standing on the corners of Via di Ripetta and Via del Babuino. With your back to the churches, take Viale G. d'Annunzio, on the right-hand side of the square.

2 Follow the road as it snakes up, turning left onto Viale Mickievicz into Giardino del Pincio (▷ 87). Continue to Piazzale Napoleone I for a view over the city. Retrace your steps to Viale del'Obelisco and turn left.

3 Carry straight on, crossing Viale del'Orologio, with its fascinating water-clock, until you reach Piazzale dei Martini and the entrance to the Villa Borghese park (▷ 87).

4 Keep walking straight along Viale delle Magnolie until you reach Via de Casina di Raffaello. Follow this road up to the 18th-century Classical Tempietto di Diana. Turn left at the temple, onto Viale dei Pupazzi.

END

PIAZZALE FLAMINIO
✛ F2 🚌 95, 120 to Piazzale Flaminio or 117, 119 to Piazza del Popolo

8 Continue straight down to Viale Washington, which ends with the spectacular gate in Piazzale Flaminio, or on the left the gate back to Piazza del Popolo.

7 Climb the steps to the Tempio di Esculapio. Take the next lane on the right to emerge onto Piazza Paolina Borghese. To leave the park, retrace your steps to Piazza Paolina Borghese, and take the road in front, Via Bernadotte, leading down to Piazzale Fiocco and the Esculapio Fountain.

6 To the right is the Museo e Galleria Borghese (▷ 79). Go left on Piazzale del Giardino Zoologico and pass the entrance to the zoo. Keep on Viale del Giardino Zoologico until you reach Largo P. Picasso.

5 When you reach Piazzale dei Cavalloi Marini, continue straight on to the end of the path.

ANTICA ENOTECA

An old-fashioned shop where you can buy wine by the bottle or glass amid trickling fountains.
🔲 G3 ✉ Via della Croce 76b ☎ 06 679 0896 🕔 Daily 11.30am–midnight

AVC DI ADRIANA CAMPANILE

Bright, modern styles for women with the distinctive red heart logo of Adriana Campanile.
🔲 G3 ✉ Piazza di Spagna 88 ☎ 06 6992 2355 🕔 Mon–Sat 10.30–7.30, Sun 11–1, 2–7.30

BATTISTONI

Traditional tailor's shop in business for over half a century. Established in 1946, clients include many celebrities.
🔲 G4 ✉ Via Condotti 61a ☎ 06 697 6111 🕔 Tue–Sat 10–7, Mon 3–7.30

ERMENEGILDO ZEGNA

Informal suits and jackets in exquisite, expensive fabrics. Also stocks shirts, sweaters and accessories.
🔲 G4 ✉ Via Borgognona 7e ☎ 06 678 9143 🕔 Mon–Sat 10–7.30, Sun 3.30–7.30

FAUSTO SANTINI

An iconoclast who designs witty, innovative and bizarre shoes.
🔲 G4 ✉ Via Frattina 120–1 ☎ 06 678 4114 🕔 Mon–Sat 10–7.30, Sun 12–7.30

FERRAGAMO

An established family firm; probably Italy's most renowned shoe shop.
🔲 G4 ✉ Via Condotti 73–4 (women's) ☎ 06 679 1565; ✉ Via Condotti 65 (men's) ☎ 06 678 1130 🕔 Mon–Sat 10–7, last Sun of month 12–7

FURLA

Chic bags, shoes, scarves and jewellery at more affordable prices than other designer names.
🔲 G3 ✉ Piazza di Spagna 22 🕔 06 692 00 363 🕔 Daily 10–8

GINORI

One of the top Italian names in modern and traditional glass and china.
🔲 G3 ✉ Piazza Trinita dei Monti 188 ☎ 06 679 3836 🕔 Tue–Sat 10–7.30

GIORGIO ARMANI

King of cut and classic,

SALES AND BARGAINS

Sales (*saldi*) in Rome are not always the bargains they seem. That said, many shoe shops and top designers cut their prices drastically during summer and winter sales (mid-Jul to mid-Sep and Jan to mid-Mar). Other lures to get you into a shop, notably the offer of *sconti* (discounts) and *vendite promozionali* (promotional offers), rarely save you any money. It can occasionally be worth asking for a discount (*uno sconto*), particularly if you are paying cash for an expensive item, or buying several items from one shop.

understated elegance.
🔲 G4 ✉ Via Condotti 77 ☎ 06 699 1460 🕔 Mon–Sat 10–7

GUCCI

Expensive, quality bags, shoes and leather goods by this famous name.
🔲 G3 ✉ Via Condotti 8 ☎ 06 679 0405 🕔 Mon–Sat 10–7, Sun 2.30–7

MARELLA

The showcase shop for the Marella label offers classic, well-made designs at reasonable prices.
🔲 G4 ✉ Via Frattina 129–31 ☎ 06 6992 3800 🕔 Tue–Sat 10–7.30, Mon, Sun 11–2, 3–7

LA PERLA

Italian lingerie is among the best in the world, and this reputation is more than upheld by La Perla.
🔲 G4 ✉ Via Condotti 78 ☎ 06 6994 1934 🕔 Tue–Sat 10–7, Mon 3–7

PINEIDER

Rome's most expensive and exclusive stationers. Virtually any design can be printed onto personalized visiting cards.
🔲 H4 ✉ Via delle Fontanell Borghese 22 ☎ 06 687 8369 🕔 Mon– Sat 10–7, Sun 10–2, 3–7

LA RINASCENTE

Chic, modern department store, good for accessories, cosmetics, designer and mid-range fashion under one roof.
🔲 K2 ✉ Piazza Fiume ☎ 06 884 1231 🕔 Daily 10–9

Entertainment and Nightlife

AUDITORIUM PARCO DELLA MUSICA
A splendid addition to Rome's classical and contemporary music scene. Three concert halls in the shape of enormous grey pods are set around a vast open-air arena.
➕ Off Map F1 ✉ Viale Pietro de Coubertin 30 ☎ 06 802411 or 06 80241281 🚌 From Stazione Termini shuttle bus M or bus/tram to Viale Tiziano 💲 Moderate

STRAVINSKIJ BAR
Picasso and the writer Jean Cocteau whiled away hours plucking

oranges from the balcony in what Cocteau described as 'heaven on earth'. This is where today's lotus eaters come to luxuriate on the terrace or in the elegant bar.
➕ G3 ✉ De Russie Hotel, Via del Babuino 9 ☎ 06 689 1694 🕐 Daily 9am–1am
Ⓜ Flaminio V

TEATRO DELL'OPERA DI ROMA
www.opera.roma.it
One of Italy's top opera houses; also an official venue for the ballet. During the summer performances are staged

outdoors in the Terme di Caracalla.
➕ J–K5 ✉ Piazza Beniamino Gigli 1 ☎ 06 4816 0255 or 06 481 7003 Ⓜ Termini
🚌 H, 40, 60, 64, 70, 71, 170 to Via Nazionale or services to Termini

TEATRO OLIMPICO
www.teatroolimpico.it
This is where the Filarmonica di Rome performs, as well as other international dance and music ensembles.
➕ Off map at F1 ✉ Piazza Gentile da Fabriano 17 ☎ 06 323 4890 Box Office 06 326 5991 🚌 225 Piazza Mancini

Restaurants

PRICES
Prices are approximate, based on a 3-course meal for one person.
€€€	over €50
€€	€30–€50
€	under €30

BRUNELLO RESTAURANT (€€€)
Dark, sleek elegance blended with Oriental touches. Chef Daniele Sera transforms the finest regional ingredients into delicious delights.
➕ H3 ✉ Via Veneto 70/A ☎ 06 4890 2867 🕐 Mon–Sat 12.30–3, 7.30–11pm Ⓜ Barberini

EST! EST! EST! (€)
Among Rome's oldest and best pizzerias.
➕ J5 ✉ Via Genova 32 ☎ 06 488 1107 🕐 Tue–Sun 6.30–11.30pm; closed Aug Ⓜ Repubblica 🚌 H, 40, 60, 64, 70, 117, 170 to Via Nazionale

RESTAURANT ETIQUETTE
Italians have a strong sense of how to behave, which applies in restaurants as much as anywhere. It is considered bad form to order only one course in more sophisticated restaurants—if that is what you want, go to a pizzeria or *trattoria*.

IL GELATO DI SAN CRISPINO (€)
Probably the best ice cream in Rome where preparation and recipes are closely guarded.
➕ H4 ✉ Via della Panetteria 42 ☎ 06 679 3924 🕐 Daily noon–12.30; closed Tue Ⓜ Barberini

LE JARDIN DE RUSSIE (€€€)
Inspired Mediterranean cuisine. Dine in the garden by candlelight for a memorable experience.
➕ G3 ✉ Via del Babuino 9 ☎ 06 3288 8870 🕐 Daily 12.30–2.30, 7.30–10.30
Ⓜ Flaminio 🚌 81, 88, 95, 117, 224, 490

Vatican City is a separate sovereign state within Rome, and home to the great basilica of St. Peter's and a series of museums with some of the world's richest and most varied collections of art and objects.

Via Plinio
Via Terenzio
Via
Via Ovidio
Boezio
Via Virgilio
Via Cassiodoro
Via Tacito
Via Orazio

CRESCENZIO

S Maria
d Carm

Via
Via Terenzio
Alberico II
PIAZZA ADRIANA
VIA
Vitelleschi
Sant'Angelo

Piazza
Cavour

VIA V COLONNA

PONTE
CAVOUR

Via Ulpiano

LUNGOTEVERE PRATI

TRIBONIANO

Piazza
Tribunali

PONTE UMBERTO I

Castel
Sant'Angelo

P

Piazza
Pia

LUNGOTEVERE VATICANO
LUNGOTEVERE CASTELLO

Ponte
Sant'Angelo

Tevere

LUNGOT IN SASSIA
PONTE VITTORIO EMANUELE II

PONTE PRINCIPE
AMEDEO SAVOIA
AOSTA

E

F

Basilica di San Pietro

TOP 25

The famous dome of St. Peter's viewed from the inside (right) and out (left)

THE BASICS

🔲 C4

✉ Piazza San Pietro, Città del Vaticano

☎ 06 6988 1662/3462

🕐 Mid-Mar–end Sep daily 7–7 (Oct–end Feb until 6). Dome Apr–end Sep 8am–5.45; Oct–end Mar 8am–4.45. Grottos Apr–end Sep daily 7–6 (Oct–end Mar until 5). Treasury Apr–end Sep daily 9–6 (Oct–end Mar until 5)

🍴 Shop

🚇 Ottaviano

🚌 64 to Porta Cavalleggeri or 23, 32, 49, 492, 990 to Piazza del Risorgimento

♿ Wheelchair access

🎟 Basilica free. Dome and Treasury moderate. Grottos expensive

HIGHLIGHTS

● St. Peter's Square and the 284 columns that suround it
● Swiss Guards
● Dome
● *Pietà*, Michelangelo
● The 2.5m (83ft) obelisk, brought from 13th-century BC Egypt in the 1st century
● *St. Peter*, Arnolfo di Cambio
● Monument to Alexander VII, Bernini

Although some of the works of art in St. Peter's can be rather disappointing, the interior impresses as the spiritual capital of Roman Catholicism with an overwhelming sense of scale and decorative glory.

The creators The first St. Peter's was built by Constantine around AD326, reputedly on the site where St. Peter was buried following his crucifixion in AD64. Between 1506 and 1626, it was virtually rebuilt to plans by Bramante, and then again to designs by Antonio da Sangallo, Giacomo della Porta, Michelangelo and Carlo Maderno. Michelangelo was also responsible for much of the dome, and Bernini finished the façade and the interior.

What to see Michelangelo's unforgettable *Pietà* (1499)—which is behind glass following an attack in 1972—is in the first chapel of the right nave. At the end of the same nave stands a statue of St. Peter: His right foot has been caressed by millions since 1857 when Pius IX granted a 50-day indulgence to anyone kissing it following confession. Bernini's high altar canopy, or *baldacchino* (1624–33), was built during the papacy of Urban VIII, a scion of the Barberini family; it is decorated with bees, the Barberini's dynastic symbol. To its rear are Guglielmo della Porta's Tomb of Paul III (left) and Bernini's influential Tomb of Urban VIII (right). Rome seen from the dome (entrance at the end of the right nave) is *the* highlight of a visit.

The route to the forti-fied castle, Ponte Sant'Angelo, watched over by Bernini's angels

Castel Sant'Angelo

Castel Sant'Angelo, rising above the river, has served as an army barracks, papal citadel, imperial tomb and medieval prison. Today the 58-room museum traces the castle's near 2,000-year history, providing a contrast to the Vatican Museums.

Many incarnations The Castel Sant'Angelo was built by Emperor Hadrian in AD130 as a mausoleum for himself, his family and his dynastic successors. It was crowned by a gilded chariot driven by a statue of Hadrian disguised as the sun god Apollo. Emperors were buried in its vaults until about AD271, when under threat of invasion from Germanic raiders it became a citadel and was incorporated into the city's walls. Its present name arose in AD590, after a vision by Gregory the Great, who while leading a procession through Rome to pray for the end of plague saw an angel sheathing a sword on this spot, an act thought to symbolize the end of the pestilence.

Castle and museum In AD847 Leo IV converted the building into a papal fortress, and in 1277 Nicholas III linked it to the Vatican by a passage-way, the *passetto*. A prison in the Renaissance, and then an army barracks after 1870, the castle became a museum in 1933. Exhibits, spread over four floors, are scattered around a confusing but fascinating array of rooms and corridors. Best of these is the beautiful Sala Paolina, done with stuc-co, fresco and *trompe-l'oeil*. The most memorable sight is the 360-degree view from the castle's ter-race, the setting for the last act of Puccini's *Tosca*.

THE BASICS

🔲 E4
✉ Lungotevere Castello 50
☎ 06 681 9111
🕐 Apr–end Sep Tue–Sun 9–7; Oct–end Mar 9–2
🍴 Café
Ⓜ Lepanto
🚌 30, 49, 70, 87, 130, 186, 224, 492, 926, 990 to Piazza Cavour or the Lungotevere
♿ Poor
💲 Expensive

HIGHLIGHTS

- Spiral funerary ramp
- Staircase of Alexander VI
- Armoury
- Hall of Justice
- Chapel of Leo X: façade by Michelangelo
- Wall paintings of Sale di Clemente VII, and its neatly decorated bathroom
- Cortile del Pozzo: wellhead
- Prisons (Prigione Storiche)
- View from Loggia of Paul III

AROUND THE VATICAN

★

TOP 25

Musei Vaticani & Cappella Sistina

The largest, richest and most impressive museum complex in the world incorporating one of Michelangelo's most supreme masterpieces in the Sistine Chapel.

Treasures of 12 museums At least two days (and 7km/4 miles of walking) are needed to do justice to the Vatican Museums. Egyptian and Assyrian art; Etruscan artefacts; the more esoteric anthropological collections; or modern religious art—whatever your priorities, several sights should not be missed. Most obvious are the four rooms of the Stanze di Raffaello, each of which is decorated with frescos by Raphael. Further fresco cycles by Pinturicchio and Fra Angelico adorn the Borgia Apartment and Chapel of Nicholas V, and are complemented by an almost unmatched collection of paintings in the Vatican Art Gallery.

Galleria della Carte Geografiche, decorated with 16th-century map frescos (far left and bottom left); Michelangelo's masterpiece, the ceiling of the Sistine Chapel (left, right and bottom right); an artefact displayed at the Vatican Museum (bottom middle)

The best of the Greek and Roman sculpture is the breathtaking Laocoön group in the Cortile Ottagono of the Museo Pio-Clementino. The list of artists whose work is shown in the Collezione di Arte Religiosa Moderna is a roll call of the most famous in the last 100 years, from Pablo Picasso to Salvador Dalí and Henry Moore.

Sistine Chapel Built by Pope Sixtus IV between 1475 and 1483, Pope Julius II commissioned Michelangelo to paint the ceiling of the Sistine Chapel in 1508. The frescos, comprising more than 300 individual figures, were completed in four years, during which Michelangelo worked in appalling conditions, lying on his back and in extremes of heat and cold. The extraordinary fresco behind the high altar, the *Last Judgment*, was begun for Pope Paul III in 1534 and completed in 1541.

THE BASICS

www.vatican.va

➕ C4

✉ Viale Vaticano, Città del Vaticano

☎ 06 6988 3322

🕐 Mar–end Oct Mon–Fri 8.45–4.45, Sat and last Sun of month 8.45–1.45; Nov–end Feb Mon–Sat and last Sun of month 8.45–1.45; closed holidays

🍴 Café, restaurant and shop

🚇 Cipro–Musei Vaticani

🚌 23, 32, 49, 81, 492, 990 to Piazza del Risorgimento, 40 to Piazza Pia or 64 to Porta Cavalleggeri

♿ Wheelchair access

💶 Very expensive (includes entry to all Vatican museums); free last Sun of month

Shopping

CASTRONI
Castroni boasts Rome's largest selection of imported delicacies, a mouthwatering array of Italian specialties and an amazing range of coffees.
🚼 D3 ✉ Via Cola di Rienzo 196, corner of Via Terenzio ☎ 06 687 4383 ⏰ Mon–Sat 8–8

FRANCHI (BENEDETTO FRANCHI)
Quite simply one of the best delicatessens in town with everything on offer from salamis, cheeses and wines to succulent roast meats and sumptuous delicacies for a picnic.
🚼 D3 ✉ Via Cola di Rienzo 200/204 ☎ 06 687 4651 ⏰ Mon–Sat 8am–9pm

MERCATO ANDREA DORIA
A large, local market that serves the area northwest of the Vatican. Stands mostly sell meat, fish, fruit and vegetables, but there are a few with shoes and quality clothes.
🚼 B3 ✉ Via Andrea Doria-Via Tunisi ⏰ Mon–Sat 7am–1pm

RELIGIOUS ARTEFACTS
For religious art and souvenirs, both serious and light-hearted, you should head to the streets around St. Peter's, notably Borgo Pio, Via del Mascherano and Via Porta di Porta Angelica.

Restaurants

PRICES
Prices are approximate, based on a 3-course meal for one person.
€€€	over €50
€€	€30–€50
€	under €30

BORGO NUOVO (€€)
Ideal after a visit to the Basilica or Vatican museums for a quiet sit down and some tasty, freshly prepared Italian food.
🚼 D4 ✉ Borgo Pio 104 ☎ 06 689 2852 ⏰ Wed–Mon 12–10 Ⓜ Ottaviano 🚌 81 to Piazza del Risorgimento

DAL TOSCANO (€–€€)
This large *trattoria* in Vatican City serves Tuscan food, and is particularly known for its meats and its wood-fired grill.
🚼 C3 ✉ Via Germanico 58/60 ☎ 06 3972 5717 ⏰ Tue–Sun 12.30–3, 8–11.15 Ⓜ Ottaviano 🚌 23, 49, 81 to Piazza del Risorgimento

LA PERGOLA (€€€)
Chef Heinz Beck's panoramic restaurant at

COFFEE
Breakfast in Rome is washed down with a cappuccino or the longer and milkier *caffè latte*. At other times espresso, a short kick-start of caffeine, is the coffee of choice or *caffé macchiato*, with a drop of milk—Italians never drink cappuccino after lunch or dinner. Decaffeinated coffee is *caffè Hag* and iced coffee *caffè freddo*.

the Cavalieri Hilton is Rome's only three Michelin-starred establishment. The elegant dining room is a splendid setting for the taster menu, which is a spectacular taste of heaven.
🚼 Off map A1 ✉ Via Cadlolo 101 ☎ 06 3509 2152 ⏰ Tue–Sat dinner only; closed 1–28 Jan, 10–25 Aug

TAVERNA ANGELICA (€€)
The best mid-priced option in the area. Delicate, innovative cooking and a minimalist interior.
🚼 D4 ✉ Piazza Amerigo Capponi 6 ☎ 06 687 4514 ⏰ Mon–Sat 7–midnight, Sun 12.30–2.30, 7.30–midnight; closed 2 weeks Aug Ⓜ Ottaviano 🚌 23 to Via San Porcari

If you're short of time, you can join an organized tour to enjoy some of the popular day trips from Rome. However, places such as the ancient ruins at Ostia Antica, can easily be made using public transport.

Ostia Antica

HIGHLIGHTS

- The Museum
- Piazalle delle Corporazioni
- The Baths of Neptune
- Casa di Diana

TIPS

- Allow a whole day for the site, perhaps bring a picnic.
- In summer, take water with you and rest in the shade during the early afternoon.
- Buy a plan of the site and spend time when you arrive planning your visit.

Imperial Rome's port is among the three best-preserved ancient towns in Italy. More than an historical treasury, Ostia's ruins invoke an intense visual sense of the past

Living history Less celebrated than Pompeii or Herculaneum, Ostia Antica more than rivals its sisters. Lying 25km (15 miles) southwest of Rome, its 4,049ha (10,000-acre) pastoral setting would do justice to Italy's most glorious country-side. Its name is Latin for 'mouth', *ostium*, referring to its location on the Tiber, and was Rome's trade-link with the outside world for 600 years—until a receding coastline and imperial decline hastened its demise. By the 17th century Ostia was all but forgotten. Legend claims its foundation in the Etruscan 7th century BC—but archaeological dating places it in the Roman 4th century BC.

The site What we see today is only about half of the town that has been uncovered by the archaeological excavations that began in the 19th century, and continue less extensively even today. Pride of place goes to the vast 4000-seat amphitheatre that is still used for open-air concerts in the summer. Though somewhat less imposing than the theatre, there are remarkable discoveries all along and leading off from the main road Decumanus Maximus, which is rutted where laden carts once carried goods to and from the great port. Set in luxuriant greenery and surrounded by Aleppo pines and cedars, there's the remains of The Forum, a 2nd century AD multi-storey apartment block called the Casa di Diana, the Baths of Neptune with its splendid mosaics—and the Piazzale della Corporazione. which is flanked by the remains of shops, offices and horrea (warehouses).

THE BASICS

www.ostia-antica.org

✚ Off map

✉ Viale di Romagnoli 717

☎ 06 5635 2830

🕐 Nov–end Feb Tue–Sun 8.30–5; Mar 8.30–6; Apr–end Oct 8.30–7 (last admission 60–90 min before closing); closed holidays

🍴 Restaurant

🚇 Metro line B to Piramide, then train from adjoining Roma–Lido station (covered by BIG ticket, ▷ 119)

♿ Moderate

More to See

CATACOMBE DI SAN CALLISTO

www.catacombe.roma.it

These 2nd-century catacombs are the largest and most impressive in Rome—and thus the most popular. They extend over 20km (12 miles) on five levels, with over 170,000 burial places. You can explore claustrophobic tunnels and numerous *loculi*, or burial niches, carved from the soft tufa stone.

✚ Off map at J9 ✉ Via Appia Antica 110/126 ☎ 06 5130 1580 or 06 513 0151 🕒 Thu–Tue 9–12, 2–5; closed Feb 🚍 714 to Piazza di S. Giovanni in Laterano, then bus 218 to Fosse Ardeatine ✋ Moderate

CATACOMBE DI SAN SEBASTIANO

Above the catacombs is the 4th-century basilica, dedicated to St. Sebastian who was martyred by arrows and where the saint was buried in the 3rd century. The catacombs themselves were some of the most important burial places in early Christian Rome, and may even have housed the bodies of saints Peter and Paul.

✚ Off map at K9 ✉ Via Appia Antica 136 ☎ 06 785 0350 🕒 Mon–Sat 8.30–12, 2.30–5.30 (5 in winter); closed part of Nov and Dec 🚍 118, 628 to Via delle Terme di Caracalla ✋ Moderate

TERME DI CARACALLA

Rome's most luxurious baths that could hold as many as 1,600 bathers. Started by Septimius Severus in AD206, and completed 11 years later by his son, Caracalla, they were designed as much as a gathering place as for hygiene. The site is now used for outdoor opera.

✚ J9 ✉ Via delle Terme di Caracalla 52 ☎ 06 575 8626 🕒 Tue–Sun 9–1 hour before sunset, Mon 9–1; closed holidays 🚇 Circo Massimo 🚍 60, 75, 81, 175, 673 to Via di San Gregorio-Via delle Terme di Caracalla ✋ Moderate (combined Appia Antica card gives admission to tombs on Via Appia Antica)

VILLA DORIA PAMPHILJ

If you have time to spare, and fancy a good long walk away from the crowds, there is nowhere better than this huge area of parkland, Rome's largest park.

✚ B8 ✉ Via di San Pancrazio 🕒 Dawn–dusk 🚍 44, 75, 870 to the Gianicolo or 115, 125 to Via Garibaldi

The finest baths ever built in Rome, Terme di Caracalla

Laid out in 1650, the gardens of Villa Doria Pamphilj

Excursions

FRASCATI

Frascati is the loveliest of the Castelli Romani towns of the Colli Albani hills, famous for its wine and dominated by a majestic villa and its gardens.

The grandest of Frascati's villas is the Villa Aldobrandini, designed in 1598 by Giacomo della Porta. The vast palace, all faded majesty, is surrounded by a superb example of an early baroque garden, from where there are fabulous views. The town is scattered with other palaces and the baroque cathedral is notable, but leave time to sample the local wine. Made here since the 3rd century BC, Frascati is a worldwide seller; it's a revelation to drink it in its birthplace.

THE BASICS

Distance: 20km (12 miles)
Journey time: 40 min
🚆 Train from Termini
🚌 COTRAL bus from Anagnina metro station
Villa Aldobrandini
✉ Via Cardinale Massaia
🕐 Garden only Apr–end Nov, Mon–Fri 9–1, 3–6; Dec–end Mar, Mon–Fri 9–1, 3–4

TIVOLI

Tivoli is the most popular excursion from Rome, thanks to the town's lovely wooded position, the superlative gardens of the Villa d'Este and the ruins and grounds of Hadrian's Roman villa.

The Este gardens were laid out in 1550 as part of a country retreat for Cardinal Ippolito d'Este, son of Lucrezia Borgia and the Duke of Ferrara. The highlights among the beautifully integrated terraces and many fountains are the hydraulic Fontana dell'Organo (Organ Fountain) that plays tunes and trumpet blasts and the Fontana della Civetta (Owl Fountain) that simulates birdsong. Hadrian's Villa (Villa Adriana) is an exceptional complex of Classical buildings, the largest ever conceived in the Roman world. It was built between AD118 and AD135 by Emperor Hadrian as an imperial palace away from the city and covered an area as great as the middle of imperial Rome.

THE BASICS

Distance: 31km (19 miles)
Journey time: 40 min
🚆 Train from Termini
🚌 COTRAL bus from Via Gaeta or metro line B to Ponte Mammolo and then COTRAL bus to Tivoli
Villa d'Este
✉ Piazza Trento
☎ 199 766 166 (call centre)
🕐 Tue–Sun 8.30–4/7.30
💶 Expensive
Villa Adriana
✉ Via di Villa Adriana–Via Tiburtina ☎ 0774 382 733
🕐 Apr–end Jan 9–5
🚌 CAT shuttle bus 4 or 4X from Tivoli centre
💶 Moderate

Entertainment and Nightlife

ALEXANDERPLATZ

www.alexanderplatz.it
Historic jazz club with live bands.

🏠 Off map ✉ Via Ostia 9
☎ 06 3974 2171 ⏰ Sep–end Jun daily 8.30pm–1.30am
Ⓜ Ottaviano 🚌 29N, 30N, 99N and 23, 70, 490, 913, 991, 994, 999 to Largo Trionfale-Viale delle Milizie 💷 4-month membership (expensive); usually free to tourists (passport required)

PIPER

Very famous club. Open since the 1960s, Piper is consistently popular, thanks partly to its schedule of constant updating.

🏠 L1 ✉ Via Tagliamento 9
☎ 06 855 5398 or 06 841 4459 ⏰ Hours erractic. Sat and Sun only in winter
🚌 63, 86, 92, N29, N30 to Via Tagliamento 💷 Very expensive

STADIO OLIMPICO

Home to Rome's two big football (soccer) teams, AS Roma and Lazio. Games are played here on alternate Sundays.

🏠 Off map ✉ Via del Foro Italico ☎ 06 323 7333 (box office) or 06 36851
Ⓜ Ottaviano. then bus 32 to Piazalle della Farnesina

AS Roma information:
Tickets available at many outlets around Rome. A full list is available on the official AS Roma website at www.asromacalcio.it. Also from Lottomatica stores and the AS Roma shop (✉ Via Colonna 360 ☎ 06 678 6514)

Lazio information:
Tickets can be bought online at www.sslazio.it. Also at Lottomatica stores or Lazio point at ✉ Via Farini ☎ 34 06 482 6768

Restaurants

PRICES

Prices are approximate, based on a 3-course meal for one person.
€€€   over €50
€€   €30–€50
€   under €30

ADRIANO (€€)

www.hoteladriano.it
Large restaurant in a 19th-century *palazzo* hotel with the same family since 1930. Classic and innovative Roman cooking, and alfresco dining.

🏠 Off map ✉ Largo M. Yourcenar 2, Tivoli ☎ 0774 382 235 ⏰ Daily 12.30–2.30, 7–10.30; closed Sun 7–10.30 winter

CACCIANI (€€)

www.cacciani.it
In business for over half a century, serving Roman and classic Italian dishes. Lovely terrace with views as far as Rome. Try the house specialty, *pollo all Romana* (chicken in the Roman manner).

🏠 Off map ✉ Via A. Diaz 13, Frascati ☎ 06 940 1991
⏰ Tue–Sun 12.30–2.30, 7–10.30; closed Sun evening Oct–end May, and 7–14 Jan, 16–26 Aug

IL GROTTINO DELLA SIBILLA DAL 1826 (€)

Well-priced, simple and tasty regional food presented in two intimate dining rooms (with a terrace for summer dining). The wine and olive oil used is home-produced.

🏠 Off map ✉ Piazza Rivarola 21, Tivoli ☎ 0774 332 606 ⏰ Tue–Sun 12.30–2.30, 7–10; closed 15 Dec–8 Jan

ZARAZÀ (€)

Appealing terrace and three attractive dining rooms, where you can enjoy traditional Roman cooking with a light touch.

🏠 Off map ✉ Via Regina Margherita 45, Frascati ☎ 06 6942 2053 ⏰ Tue–Sun 12.30–2.30, 7–10.30; closed Sun 7–10.30 Oct–end May and part of Aug

Rome has a vast range of hotels in every price category, including some of Italy's most prestigious establishments. Many hotels are over-priced and poorly located; if you are on a short visit it pays to choose a hotel in or close to the historic area.

Introduction

Following Rome's renaissance in the wake of the Jubilee Year in 2000, the number of luxury five-star hotels in the city is now almost double what it was. Previously crumbling *palazzi* and many of the longer-established hotels have been restored.

Location, Location

As in any city, Rome has a wide range of accommodation types, from small, low-budget places around the Termini to grand, five-star luxury establishments on the Via Veneto. What to expect in terms of price and quality depends largely on location. Staying in the *centro storico* means that you are close to all of Rome's sights, but also to its sounds. Narrow streets and tall buildings tend to amplify the noise. Quiet places can be found, on the edge of the popular areas or in hotels with double glazing. If you really value your sleep, book a room in the quieter Aventino, Celio or Prati districts. The disadvantage here is that you will have to travel, but public transport is inexpensive, and hotels are often cheaper than in the heart of the city.

What You Get For your Money

The familiar star system operates in Italy, with five stars denoting the highest standard of comfort, luxury and facilities. A one-star hotel has few facilities and frequently does not include a private bathroom. Normally both television and telephone will be in the lobby. These establishments tend not to accept credit cards and do not have a 24-hour desk service.

RESERVATIONS

As Rome is an eternally popular destination, it pays to reserve well in advance, especially if your stay is over the peak periods, which, nowadays, tend to be the greater part of the year. However, January to March and August are the least crowded months and you should be able to get some deals in this period. Consult hotel websites for details of special offers. If you arrive without a reservation, do ask to see the room first before you commit. Information agencies are always a useful resource.

After a hectic day sight-seeing, its nice to come back to a welcome smile and home comforts

Budget Hotels

PRICES

Expect to pay up to €150 per night for a double room in a budget hotel.

58 LE REAL DE LUXE

www.58viacavour.it
B&B with attention to detail. The 16 rooms are beautifully furnished, combining gleaming bedsteads with crystal chandeliers and leather armchairs with plasma-screen TV and big walk-in showers.
✚ K5 ✉ Via Cavour 58 ☎ 06 482 3566 Ⓜ Cavour or Station Termini

B&B 3 COINS

Three coins and three wishes for this modest but welcoming B&B round the corner from the Trevi Fountain. Seven bedrooms vary in size, are pleasantly furnished and have good facilities.
✚ G4 ✉ Via dei Crociferi 26 ☎ 06 446 0434; fax 06 446 0434 🚌 Many services to Via del Tritone

HOTEL & HOSTEL DES ARTISTES

www.hoteldesartistes.com
There's a choice here between hostel-style basic accommodation or good amenities in the three-star hotel. Both have access to a rooftop terrace.
✚ L4 ✉ Via Villafranca 20 ☎ 06 445 4365 Ⓜ Castro Pretorio

HOTEL TRASTEVERE

www.hoteltrastevere.net
Twenty bright rooms, all with private bathrooms, plus four apartments.
✚ E7 ✉ Via Luciano Manara 24 ☎ 06 581 4713; fax 06 588 1016 🚌 H, 8, 780 to Piazza S. Sonnino or Viale Trastevere

NAVONA

www.hotelnavona.com
Twenty-six simple rooms, friendly owners and a superb central location, in a 15th-century *palazzo*.
✚ F5 ✉ Via dei Sediari 8 ☎ 06 686 4203; fax 06 6880 3802 🚌 30, 70, 87, 116, 186 to Corso del Rinascimento

PERUGIA

www.hperugia.it
Little-known, quiet and well placed between the Colosseum and Via Cavour; very convenient for the sights of the

NOISE

Noise is a fact of life in every Roman hotel, whatever the price category. Surveys have shown Rome to be the noisiest city in Europe. It is difficult to escape the cacophony entirely (unless the hotel is air-conditioned and windows are double-glazed), but to lessen the potential racket you should avoid rooms overlooking main thoroughfares and the area around Termini in favour of rooms looking out on parks or obscure back streets. Also ask for rooms away from the front of the hotel or facing on to a central courtyard (*cortile*).

Ancient City. All 11 rooms have private bathrooms.
✚ J6 ✉ Via del Colosseo 7 ☎ 06 679 7200; fax 06 678 4635 🚌 75, 84, 117 to Via Cavour or 75, 85, 87, 117, 175 to the Colosseum

POMEZIA

www.hotelpomezia.it
Close to Piazza Navona with 17 small rooms (some have private bathrooms). Roof terrace and small bar. Specially adapted room for people with disabilities but no lift.
✚ F6 ✉ Via dei Chiavari 12 ☎ 06 686 1371; fax 06 686 1371 🚌 46, 62, 64 to Corso Vittorio Emanuele II or 8, 46, 62, 63, 64, 70, 80 to Largo di Torre Argentina

SMERALDO

www.hotelsmeraldoroma.com
Thirty-five plain and clean rooms. In a back street close to Campo de' Fiori.
✚ F6 ✉ Vicolo dei Chiodaroli 11 ☎ 06 687 5929; fax 06 6880 5495 🚌 46, 62, 64 to Corso Vittorio Emanuele II or 8, 46, 62, 63, 64, 70, 80 to Largo di Torre Argentina

SOLE

www.solealbiscione.it
A popular choice on the edge of Campo de' Fiori, this is Rome's oldest hotel dating back to 1462, with 59 rooms and a small garden terrace.
✚ F6 ✉ Via del Biscione 76 ☎ 06 6880 6873; fax 06 689 3787 🚌 46, 62, 64 to Corso Vittorio Emanuele II or 8, 46, 62, 63, 64, 70, 80 to Largo di Torre Argentina

Mid-Range Hotels

PRICES

Expect to pay between €150 and €300 per night for a double room in a mid-range hotel.

ABRUZZI

www.hotelabruzzi.it
Twenty-five large rooms (and eight shared bathrooms), some with a view of the Pantheon; rooms at the rear are quieter.
🔲 F5 ✉ Piazza della Rotonda 69 ☎ 06 679 2021; fax 06 6978 8076; 🚌 119 to Piazza della Rotonda or 46, 62, 63, 64, 70, 87, 186 to Largo di Torre Argentina

ALBERGO CESARI

www.albergocesari.it
Friendly and straightforward three-star hotel with a loyal clientele and 47 elegant rooms and a fabulous roof garden/terrace. Very long established—there has been a hotel here since 1787. Excellent position at the heart of the historic city.
🔲 G5 ✉ Via di Pietra 89a ☎ 06 674 9701; fax 06 6749 7030 🚌 60, 62, 85, 117, 119, 160 to Via del Corso

BOLIVAR

www.bolivarhotel.com
This three-star hotel is perfectly positioned for sights of the Ancient City, in a quiet alley just off busy Via IV Novembre. 30 spacious, recently renovated rooms. Breakfast is taken on the roof terrace.
🔲 H6 ✉ Via della Cordonata 6, between Via IV Novembre and Via XXIV Maggio ☎ 06 679 1614; fax 06 679 1025
🚌 Barberini 🚌 H, 40, 60, 64, 70, 116T, 117, 170 to Via IV Novembre or Via Nazionale

CAMPO DE' FIORI

www.hotelcampodefiori.com
Good value and position close to Campo de' Fiori. The 27 rooms are rather small and vary in decor, from exposed brick to funky red and green colours. The roof garden is a pleasant bonus.
🔲 F6 ✉ Via del Biscione 6 ☎ 06 6880 6865; fax 06 687 6003 🚌 46, 62, 64 to Corso Vittorio Emanuele II

CASA HOWARD

www.casahoward.com
Split into two houses, both near the Piazza di Spagna, this boutique hotel offers 10 stylish rooms. The location is excellent for shopping and the sights near the Spanish Steps and Fontana di Trevi.
🔲 G4 ✉ Via Capo le Case 18 ☎ 06 6992 4555; fax 06 6794 6444 🚇 Spagna

AGENCIES

Two good sources for all kinds of accommodation, from hotels to bed-and-breakfast in all price ranges, are the Hotel Reservation Agency (☎ 06 699 1000; www.hotelreservation.it) and Enjoy Rome (☎ 06 445 1843 or 06 445 0734; www.enjoyrome.com ⏰ Mon–Fri 8.30–7, Sat 8.30–2).

🚌 116, 116T, 117, 119, 590 to Via dei Due Macelli or all services to Via del Tritone

CELIO

www.hotelcelio.com
Enviable spot in front of the Colosseum, this stylish yet funky hotel offers 19 spacious rooms, each distinguished by large frescos of Renaissance themes. Rooms on the upper floor have Jacuzzis.
🔲 J7 ✉ Via dei Santissimi Quattro 35/c ☎ 06 7049 5333; fax 06 709 6377 🚇 Colosseo

DUE TORRI

www.hotelduetorriroma.com
A real find, in a perfect position hidden in a tiny alley between Piazza Navona and the Tiber. The 26 adequate rooms vary from stylish to plain. Some have small terraces with good views.
🔲 F5 ✉ Vicolo del Leonetto 23–25 ☎ 06 687 6983; fax 06 686 5442 🚌 30, 70, 81, 87, 116, 186 to Lungotevere Marzio or Corso del Rinascimento

HOTEL MODIGLIANI

www.hotelmodigliani.com
Round the corner from the Via Veneto, this charming hotel has many artistic touches. There are 23 spacious, airy rooms, an inner courtyard and the superior rooms on the top floor have splendid views over Rome.
🔲 H4 ✉ Via della Purificaziione 42 ☎ 06 4281 5226; fax 06 4281 4791 🚇 Barberini

WHERE TO STAY MID-RANGE HOTELS

HOTEL PORTOGHESI
www.hotelportoghesiroma.com
A well-known hotel in a baroque *palazzo* with a roof terrace. Has been updated while retaining the 19th-century period feel of its 27 rooms. In a cobbled street north of Piazza Navona.
➕ F4 ✉ Via dei Portoghesi 1
☎ 06 686 4231; fax 06 687 6976 🚌 30, 70, 87, 116 to Corso del Rinascimento

HOTEL QUIRINALE
www.hotelquirinale.it
Composers such as Puccini and Verdi have stayed at the charming Quirinale—a private connecting door offers privileged access to the Opera House. High-ceiling rooms are sensitively refurbished in the classical style, with chandeliers, parquet floors, early empire furnishings and huge bathrooms. Breakfast in the shaded loggia overlooking the courtyard is a delight.
➕ J4 ✉ Via Nazionale 7
☎ 06 4707; fax 06 4820 099
🚇 Repubblica

LOCARNO
www.hotellocarno.com
In a quietish side street close to Piazza del Popolo. Much genuine 1920s art nouveau decor, but with a feel of old-world elegance plus nice touches such as an open fire in winter and a garden and roof terrace. Ask for the better rooms in the eastern annexe,

not the downbeat rooms in the main building.
➕ F3 ✉ Via della Penna 22
☎ 06 361 0841; fax 06 321 5249 🚇 Flaminio 🚌 926 to Via di Ripetta, or 81 to Lungotevere in Augusta

MANFREDI
www.hotelmanfredi.it
Quiet family-run hotel with charming service and 18 pretty rooms, in a cobbled street of galleries and antiques shops.
➕ G3 ✉ Via Margutta 61
☎ 06 320 7676; fax 06 320 7736 🚇 Spagna 🚌 119 to Piazza di Spagna

NERVA
www.hotelnerva.com
Unbeatable position for

RESERVATIONS

Rome's peak season runs from Easter to October, but the city's hotels (in all categories) are almost invariably busy. Telephone, write or fax well in advance to reserve a room (most receptionists speak some English, French or German). Leave a credit card number or send an international money order for the first night's stay to be certain of the booking. Reconfirm a few days before your trip. If you arrive without a reservation then get to a hotel early in the morning; by afternoon most vacated rooms will have been snapped up. Don't accept rooms from touts at Stazione Termini.

the sights of the Ancient City—this is one of only a few hotels within a stone's throw of the Roman Forum. Renovated rooms, some with original features, amiable service and a warm welcome.
➕ H6 ✉ Via Tor de'Conti 3
☎ 06 678 1835; fax 06 6992 2204 🚇 Colosseo or Cavour 🚌 60, 84, 85, 87, 175 and all other services to Via dei Fori Imperiali, Piazza Venezia or Via IV Novembre-Via Nazionale

LA RESIDENZA
www.hotel-la-residenza.com
Good choice, close to Via Vittorio Veneto (but away from the hustle and bustle) and reasonably priced for this expensive area. Combines the luxury of an affordable five-star hotel with the intimacy and easy going charm of a private house. Terrace and roof garden. 25 rooms.
➕ H3 ✉ Via Emilia 22–24
☎ 06 488 0789; fax 06 485721 🚇 Barberini 🚌 52, 53, 80, 95, 116, 119 to Via Vittorio Veneto

LA RESIDENZA FARNESE
www.residenzafarneseroma.it
A superb position in an ivy-hung alley and in the shadow of the great Palazzo Farnese. Part of a former convent, the rooms vary from modest former nuns' cells with small bathrooms to large, pastel-decorated salons.
➕ E6 ✉ Via del Mascherone 59 ☎ 06 6821 0980; fax 06 8032 1049 🚌 116, 116T to Via Giulia and Via dei Farnesi

Luxury Hotels

PRICES

Expect to pay over €300 per night for a double room in a luxury hotel.

CAPO D'AFRICA
www.hotelcapodafrica.com
In the shadow of the Colosseum, this designer boutique hotel boasts sleek contemporary, with sunny, bright shades and displays of Italian modern art. Roof terrace.

➕ K7 ✉ Via Capo d'Africa 54 ☎ 06 772801; fax 06 77 280801 Ⓜ Colosseo

DE RUSSIE
www.roccofortehotels.com
A glorious hotel just off Piazza del Popolo that is distinguished by its modern and stylish design. The 122 rooms are calm and bright, and most have views of the delightful gardens, a lovely spot to dine alfresco.

➕ F3 ✉ Via del Babuino 9 ☎ 06 328 881; fax 3288 8888 Ⓜ Flaminio 🚌 117, 119 to Piazza del Popolo

HASSLER-VILLA MEDICI
www.hotelhasslerroma.com
Well-located longtime jet-set and VIP haunt, just above the Spanish Steps. 95 rooms and 8 suites.

➕ H4 ✉ Piazza Trinità dei Monti 6 ☎ 06 699 340; fax 06 678 9991 Ⓜ Spagna 🚌 119 to Piazza di Spagna

HOTEL ART
www.hotelart.it
A long minimalist white marble corridor provides access to the entrance hall of this latest addition to the glamorous Spanish Steps area. High-tech furnishings and bright hues blend with parquet floors and hand-stiched leather. The bathrooms feature glass, metal and mosaic tiles.

➕ G3 ✉ Via Margutta 56 ☎ 06 328 711; fax 06 3600 3995 Ⓜ Spagna

LORD BYRON
www.lordbyronhotel.com
Small, refined and very chic in leafy Parioli. Noted for its excellent restaurant Relais Le Jardin. 26 rooms, plus 6 suites.

➕ G1 ✉ Via Giuseppe de Notaris 5 ☎ 06 322 0404; fax 06 322 0405 Ⓜ Flaminio 🚌 52 to Via Bruno Buozzi

RAPHAËL
www.raphaelhotel.com
Intimate, charming and ivy covered—hidden away yet near Piazza Navona. The 55 rooms are elegantly furnished with classic taste. Reserve ahead.

➕ F5 ✉ Largo Febo 2 ☎ 06 682 831; fax 06 687 8993 🚌 70, 81, 87 to Corso del Rinascimento

REGINA HOTEL BAGLIONI
www.reginabaglioni.hotelinroma.com
Murano glass chandeliers, silk tapestries and marble bathrooms are just some of the luxury fixtures and fittings in this lovely Liberty-style hotel. The Sala Belvedere on the eighth floor has glass walls and a large sunroof with splendid views. Service and attention to detail are exemplary.

➕ H3 ✉ Via Vittorio Veneto 72 ☎ 06 421 111; fax 06 4201 2130 Ⓜ Barberini

ST. REGIS GRAND
www.stregis.com
Not in the most salubrious or convenient spot, but immensely lavish and luxurious. 153 rooms, plus 8 suites.

➕ K4 ✉ Via Vittorio Emanuele Orlando 3 ☎ 06 47091/474 709; fax 06 4709 2831 Ⓜ Repubblica 🚌 H, 40, 170, 492, 910 to Piazza della Repubblica

WHAT TO PAY

Hotels are classified by the Italian state into five categories from one star (basic) to five stars (luxury). The prices each can charge are set by law and must be displayed in the room (you will usually find them on the door). However, prices within a hotel can vary from room to room (and some hotels have off- and peak-season rates). If a room is too expensive, do not be afraid to ask for a less expensive one. Watch for extras like air-conditioning and obligatory breakfasts. Single rooms cost about two-thirds the price of doubles, and to have an extra bed in a room adds 35 per cent to the bill.

Rome can be a busy and intimidating place, but behind the bustle it is easy to access the city from its two airports, while public transport, on the few occasions you will need it, is reliable and straightforward.

Getting There   116–117

Getting Around   118–119

Essential Facts   120–121

Language   122–123

Timeline   124–125

Planning Ahead

When to Go

The best time to visit Rome is April to early June or mid-September to October, when the weather is not uncomfortably hot. Easter weekend is very busy. Many restaurants and businesses close for the entire month of August. January and February are the quietest months.

TIME

Italy is one hour ahead of GMT in winter, six hours ahead of New York and nine hours ahead of Los Angeles.

AVERAGE DAILY MAXIMUM TEMPERATURES

JAN	FEB	MAR	APR	MAY	JUN	JUL	AUG	SEP	OCT	NOV	DEC
44°F	46°F	52°F	58F	64°F	74°F	79°F	77°F	72°F	64°F	55°F	48°F
7°C	8°C	11°C	14°C	18°C	23°C	26°C	25°C	22°C	18°C	13°C	9°C

Spring (March to April) can be muggy and rainy in April and May.
Summer (June to August) is hot and dry, with sudden thunderstorms. July and August are uncomfortably hot.
Autumn (September to November) is mixed but can produce crisp days with clear skies.
Winter (December to February) is short and cold.

WHAT'S ON

January *La Befana* (6 Jan): Epiphany celebrations; fair and market in Piazza Navona.
February *Carnevale* (week before Lent): Costume festivities; parties on Shrove Tuesday.
March *Festa di San Giuseppe* (19 Mar): Street stalls in the Trionfale area north of the Vatican.
April *Good Friday* (Mar/Apr): Procession of the Cross at 9pm to the Colosseum, led by the Pope.
Easter Sunday: The Pope addresses the crowds at noon in Piazza di San Pietro.

May *International Horse Show* (early May): Concorso Ippico in Villa Borghese.
June *Festa della Repubblica* (2 Jun): Military parade along Via de' Fiori Imperiali.
July *Tevere Expo* (last week Jun/Jul): Food and handicrafts fair on the banks of the Tiber.
August *Ferragosto* (15 Aug): Feast of the Assumption; everything closes.
September *Art Fair*: Via Margutta.
Sagra dell'Uva (early Sep): Wine and harvest festival in the Basilica di Massenzio.

October *Antiques Fair* (mid-Oct): Via dei Coronari.
November *Ognissanti* (1–2 Nov): All Saints' Day.
Festa di Santa Cecilia (22 Nov): In the catacombs and church of Santa Cecilia in Trastavere.
December *Festa della Madonna Immacolata* (8 Dec): Pope and other dignitaries leave flowers at the statue of the Madonna in Piazza di Spagna.
Christmas Eve Midnight Mass: Most striking are at Santa Maria Maggiore and Santa Maria in Aracoeli.

Useful Websites

www.romaturismo.it
Rome's official website for tourist information, has mostly generalized information on the city.

www.adr.it
The official site of Rome's main airports, Fiumincino and Ciampino, with useful contacts and details of transport links to the city.

www.vatican.va
Vatican City's polished official website offers multilingual information on the Musei Vaticani, a calendar of religious events, an online version of its official newspaper and other general information on the Vatican.

www.comune.roma.it
Aimed primarily at tourists, the official website of Rome's city council contains transport and other useful general information.

www.romaclick.com
A general site useful for checking up-to-the-minute information on events and exhibitions. It offers a user-friendly accommodation reservation service with last-minute reductions.

www.romeguide.it
An Italian-based site with a wealth of daily updated information; use it for reserving museum passes and to find out what's on.

www.enjoyrome.com
This friendly English-language site is run from Rome and has a quirkier approach than most; use it for general information, as well as tips on discovering Rome on foot and by public transport. Excellent links and daily updates.

www.museionline.it
Informative and easy-to-navigate site that will fill you in on what the city's museums have to offer. Lots of practical information as well. Opening times and prices are not always current.

PRIME TRAVEL SITES

www.atac.roma.it
Rome's bus company website gives every scrap of information about public transport, including maps and how to buy the best ticket for your needs—Italian and English.

www.capitolium.org
Devoted to the Roman Forum and the Imperial Fora, this site includes a wide range of historical material, including reconstructions of how the Fora might have looked in its original state.

www.catacombe.roma.it
The official site of Rome's catacombs.

www.fodors.com
A travel-planning site where you can research prices and weather, book tickets, cars and rooms, and ask questions; links to other sites.

CYBERCAFÉS

easyInternetcafe
www.easyinternetcafe.com
✉ H4 ✉ Via Barberini 2
🕐 Daily 7am–1am

Globalservice
✉ F7 ✉ Piazza S. Sonnino 27 ☎ 06 5833 3316
🕐 Daily 8am–midnight

Getting There

VISAS AND INSURANCE

Check visa and passport requirements before travelling, see www.britishembassy.gov.uk or www.american embassy.com. EU citizens are covered for medical expenses with an EHIC card; insurance to cover illness and theft is still strongly advised. Visitors from outside the EU should check their insurance coverage and, if necessary, buy a supplementary policy.

TIPS

● Avoid taxi and hotel touts who will approach you at the airport. Use only licensed (yellow or white) taxis.
● Buy your return (round-trip) train ticket when you arrive at Fiumicino. The queues are much longer at Termini, and the ticket will not become valid until you stamp it on your return journey.
● You will find suitcases with wheels a godsend at Fiumicino. It is quite some distance between baggage reclaim and the exit, and for some stretches you cannot use a baggage trolley, particularly on the homeward journey.

AIRPORTS

There are direct flights into Rome from Europe and North America to Leonardo da Vinci and Ciampino airports. Visitors from Europe can also arrive by rail to Stazione Termini, or by bus.

60KM (37 miles)

Leonardo da Vinci Airport
36km (22 miles) to city centre
Train 45 min, €9.50

Ciampino Airport
15km (9 miles) to city centre
Bus/Metro 35 min

FROM LEONARDO DA VINCI

Scheduled flights arrive at this airport 36km (22 miles) southwest of the city, better known as Fiumicino (☎ switchboard 06 65951, 24hr recorded 06 6593 3640, flight information 06 6563 4956 (international), 06 65643 (domestic). The website for both main Rome airports is www.adr.it. The most economical way to reach the heart of Rome from the airport is by rail into Stazione Termini. Trains leave every 30 or 60 minutes (6.37am–11.37pm) at 7 and 37 minutes past the hour and take about 35 minutes. Buses depart outside train hours and take up to 50 minutes to Rome's Termini and Tiburtina train stations. Taxis take from 30 minutes to two hours depending on traffic, and are expensive (€40–€55). Take only licensed cabs (white or yellow) or a prepaid car with driver available from the SOCAT desk in the International Arrivals hall.

FROM CIAMPINO

This smaller airport, which handles mostly low-cost and charter flights, is 15km (9 miles) southeast of the city. There are good facilities but the airport doesn't have a direct rail link to the heart of Rome. To get there take a 15-minute bus journey by COTRAL bus to the Metro (underground) station at Anagnina, then the 20-minute journey to Termini on Metro line A. Taxis take between 30 and 40 minutes and cost around €40. Bus shuttles (☎ 06 7949 4572; www.terravision.it) serve various no-frills and other airlines' flights and run to Termini (€8 one-way, €14 round-trip). Terravision also operates from Fiumicino airport to Termini (€7 one-way, €12 round-trip).

ARRIVING BY BUS

Most long-distance buses terminate at Tiburtina, to the northeast of the city. Although the station is somewhat way out of the city, it is well served by the Metro (line B) and by numerous bus services (for example. No. 492). Eurolines run buses from more than 100 European cities. For details of routes and tickets, see their website (www.eurolines.com).

ARRIVING BY CAR

In the days of the empire, all roads led to Rome, but in these modern times, all roads lead to the Gran Raccordo Anulare, known as the GRA. This 70km (43-mile) road encircles the city, and is always busy. From Fiumicino airport, take the Autostrada Roma Fiumicino, which leads to the GRA. If you are coming from Ciampino you will need to follow the Via Appia Nuova. From Florence or Pisa, take the A1, also known as the Autostrada del Sole. Visitors arriving from Naples should also use the A1, while those coming from Abruzzo or the Adriatic coast should follow the A24. Wherever you join the GRA, make sure you know which exit you need; your hotel can tell you which one is best.

ARRIVING BY RAIL

Most trains arrive and depart from Stazione Termini, which is convenient for most of central Rome. Taxis and buses leave from the station forecourt, Piazza dei Cinquecento. Train information ☎ 8488 88088; www.trenitalia.com.

DRIVING PERMIT

If you are arriving by car and staying in central Rome, you will need a permit to drive in the city. If you are staying in a hotel, the staff can arrange this.

LONG-TERM PARKING

If you are arriving by car, but don't want to use your car in Rome, you can leave it in the long-term parking area (*lungo sosta parcheggio*) at Fiumicino airport and take the train into the city. Parking costs €18 for 24 hours or €69 for seven days. Short-stay costs €28 daily (☎ 06 6595 5175).

CAR RENTAL

All major rental firms, and some local ones, have desks at both airports and also in town. Car rental is expensive in Italy and you can often get a better deal if you arrange it before you leave home. The minimum age for renting a car is between 21 and 25 (depending on which company), and you will need a have held a driver's licence for a least a year. Most firms require a credit card as a deposit. Accident rates are high in Rome, so make sure you have adequate insurance cover. Most car rental contracts include breakdown cover.

Getting Around

NEED TO KNOW GETTING AROUND

AMERICAN EXPRESS

American Express runs bus tours around Rome and farther afield. It also organizes three- to four-hour walks of the city with English-speaking guides. Reserve ahead at busy times (✉ Piazza di Spagna 38 ☎ 06 67642 🕐 Apr–end Sep, Mon–Fri 9–5.30, Sat 9–3; Oct–end Mar, Mon–Fri 9–5.30, Sat 9–12.30 🚌 119 to Piazza di Spagna).

VISITORS WITH DISABILITIES

Rome is not an easy place for visitors with physical disabilities. However, Vatican City has ramps and elevators and some hotels have rooms for visitors with disabilities. Staff at airports, museums and places of interest are willing to help and taxis usually accept wheel-chairs, although it is a good idea to phone ahead. The B line Metro is generally accessible (apart from Circo Massimo, Colosseo and Cavour) but the A line and most buses are not. For details contact RADAR (✉ Unit 12, City Forum, 250 City Road, London ECU 8AF ☎ 020 7250 3222; www.radar.org.uk) in the UK or Society for the Advancement of Travel and Hospitality (SATH) (✉ 347 5th Avenue, Suite 610 NY 10016 ☎ 212/447 7284; www.sath.org) in the US.

BUSES

Service is frequent and inexpensive on Rome's orange, green or red-grey regional and blue suburban buses run by ATAC/COTRAL 🚏 K4 ✉ Piazza dei Cinquecento ☎ 800 431784 (freephone) or 06 4695 2057; www.atac.roma.it 🕐 Mon–Fri 9–1, plus Tue and Fri 2.30–5 🚇 Termini
The buses are often crowded and slow. Buy BIT tickets (*Biglietto Integrato a Tempo*; €1) before boarding, from tobacconists, shops and automatic machines displaying an ATAC sticker. Your ticket must be stamped at the rear of the bus or tram, and is valid for any number of bus rides and one Metro ride within the next 75 minutes. Day (€4) and three-day (€11) BTI passes are available. These need only be validated the first time they are used. Services run 5.30am–11.30pm, depending on the route. The night service consists of buses on key routes midnight–5.30am; night buses have a conductor selling tickets. Remember to enter buses by back doors and to leave by middle doors (if you have a pass or validated ticket with unexpired time you can also use the front doors). Buy several tickets at once as some outlets close early or the 5-ticket 5BIT-Multibit pass (€5), which must be validated for each journey. There are large fines if you are caught without a ticket. Bus stops (*fermate*) list routes and bus numbers and note that one-way streets often force buses to return along different routes. Note that bus number 64 is especially notorious for pickpockets.

USEFUL SERVICES

- 23 Piazza del Risorgimento (for the Vatican Museums)–Trastevere–Piramide
- 75 Termini–Roman Forum–Colosseum–Piramide
- 40, 64 Termini–Piazza Venezia–close to Piazza San Pietro/St. Peter's
- 110 Sightseeing service from Stazione Termini and other key monuments
- 81 Piazza del Risorgimento (Vatican

Museums)–Piazza Venezia
● 117, 119 Circular minibus service in the historic centre: Piazza Augusto Imperatore–Piazza della Rotonda (Pantheon)–Via del Corso–Piazza di Spagna
● 780 Piazza Venezia–Trastevere

SUBWAY
Rome's subway, the Metro, has two lines, A and B, which intersect at Stazione Termini. Mainly a commuter service and of limited use in the city, it is good for trans-city rides. Station entrances are marked by a large M and each displays a map of the network. Services run 5.30am to 11.30pm (12.30am Saturday). Tickets are valid for one ride and can be bought from tobacconists, bars and shops displaying ATAC or COTROL stickers, and from machines at stations—have euro coins handy.

TAXIS
Official taxis are yellow or white, with a 'Taxi' sign on the roof. Use only these and refuse touts at Fiumicino, Termini and elsewhere. Drivers are not supposed to stop on the streets so it is difficult to hail a cab. Taxis congregate at stands, indicated by blue signs printed with 'Taxi'. Make sure the meter is reset when you start your journey (note one part of the meter will display the minimum-fare starting rate). Ranks are available in the area at Termini, Piazza S Sonnino, Pantheon, Piazza di Spagna and Piazza San Silvestro.
Calling a taxi: the company will give you a taxi code name, a number and the time it will take to get to you. The meter starts running as soon as they are called. Companies include: Samaranda ☎ 06 5551; Autoradio Taxi ☎ 06 3570; Capitale Radio ☎ 06 4994. The minimum fare is valid for 3km (2.5 miles) or the first 9 minutes of a ride. Surcharges are levied between 10pm and 7am, all day Sunday, on national holidays, for airport trips and for each piece of luggage larger than 35 x 25 x 50cm (13 x 9 x 19in).

HANDY HINT
An integrated ticket, the *Biglietto Integrato Giornaliero* (BIG) is valid for a day's unlimited travel on ATAC buses, the Metro, COTRAL buses and suburban trains (except to Fiumicino airport). The *Carta Integrata Settimanale* pass (€16) is valid for a week as for BIG tickets (see above).

LOST PROPERTY
Report lost or stolen property to a police station, which will issue a signed declaration for your insurance company. The central police station is the Questura
✉ Via San Vitale 15
☎ 06 46861 (tourist department) or ☎ 06 4686 2102
ATAC lost property
✉ Via Niccolò Bettoni 1
☎ 06 581 6040
🕐 Mon–Sat 8.30–1
Metro lost property
Line A ☎ 06 487 4309;
Line B ☎ 06 5735 2264
🕐 Mon, Wed, Fri 9–12
COTRAL lost property
Inquire at the route's origin or telephone ☎ 06 57531 or 06 591 5551
Rail lost property
✉ Stazione Termini, Via Giovanni Giolitti 24 ☎ 06 4782 5543 🕐 Mon–Fri 7am–10pm
Airport lost property
☎ 06 6595 3343 🕐 Mon–Fri 9–1, also Thu 2–3.30

Essential Facts

- 1 Jan (New Year's Day)
- 6 Jan (Epiphany)
- Easter Monday
- 25 Apr
- 1 May (Labour Day)
- 29 Jun (St. Peter & St. Paul's Day)
- 15 Aug (Assumption)
- 1 Nov (All Saints' Day)
- 8 Dec (Immaculate Conception
- 25 Dec (Christmas Day)
- 26 Dec (St. Stephen's Day)

MONEY

The euro is the official currency of Italy. Banknotes come in denominations of 5, 10, 20, 50, 100, 200 and 500 euros and coins in 1, 2, 5, 10, 20, 50 cents and 1 and 2 euros.

10 euros

50 euros

200 euros

500 euros

ELECTRICITY
- Current is 220 volts AC, 50 cycles; plugs are the two-round-pin type.

NEWSPAPERS & MAGAZINES
- Most Romans read the Rome-based *Il Messaggero*, the mainstream and authoritative *Corriere della Sera* or the middle-left and popularist *La Repubblica* (which has a special Rome edition). Sports papers (such as *Corriere dello Sport*) and news magazines (like *Panorama* and *L'Espresso*) are also popular.
- Foreign newspapers can usually be bought after 2.30pm on the day of issue from booths (*edicole*) on and close to Termini, Piazza Colonna, Largo di Torre Argentina, Piazza Navona, Via Vittoria Veneto and close to several tourist sights. European editions of the *International Herald Tribune*, *USA Today* and the *Financial Times* are also available.

OPENING HOURS
- Shops: Tue–Sat 8–1, 4–8, Mon 4–8 (with seasonal variations) or, increasingly Mon/Tue–Sat 9.30–7.30. Food shops open on Monday morning but may close on Thursday afternoon.
- Restaurants: daily 12.30–3, 7.30–10.30. Many close on Sunday evening and half- or all day Monday. Most bars and restaurants also have a statutory closing day (*riposo settimanale*) and many close for much of August.
- Churches: variable, but usually daily 7–12, 4.30–7. Most churches close Sunday afternoon.
- Museums and galleries: vary considerably; usually close on Monday.
- Banks: Mon–Fri 8.30–1.30. Major branches may also open 3–4 and Saturday morning.
- Post offices: Mon–Fri 8.15 or 9–2; Sat 8.15 or 9–12 or 2

POSTAL SERVICE
- Buy stamps from post offices and tobacconists.
- Post boxes are red and have two slots, one for Rome (marked *Per La Città*) and one for other destinations (*Per Tutte Le Altre*

Destinazioni). New boxes, usually blue, are for the priority mail service, or *Posta Priorita*.

● Vatican post can be posted only in the Vatican's blue *Poste Vaticane* post boxes. The Vatican postal service is quicker (although tariffs are the same), but stamps can be bought only at the post offices in the Vatican Museums ⓞ Mon–Fri 8.30–7 and in Piazza San Pietro ☎ 06 6988 3406 ⓞ Mon–Fri 8.30–7, Sat 8.30–6

● Main post office (*Ufficio Postale Centrale*) ✉ Piazza San Silvestro 18–20 ☎ 06 6771; www.poste.it ⓞ Mon–Fri 9am–6.30/7.30pm, Sat 8.30–1 (9–12 last Sat of month).

TELEPHONES

● Telephone numbers listed in this book include the city area code (06), which must be dialled even when calling from within Rome.
● Public telephones are indicated by a red or yellow sign showing a telephone dial and receiver. They are found on the street, in bars and restaurants and in special offices (*Centri Telefoni*) equipped with banks of phones.
● Phones usually accept phone cards (*schede telefoniche*) available from tobacconists, post offices and some bars in a variety of denominations. Break off the card's corner before use.
● To call Italy from the UK, dial 00 44 and from the US or Canada dial 011, followed by 39 (the country code for Italy) then the number, including the relevant city code.

TOURIST INFORMATION

● Azienda di Promozione Turistica di Roma ✉ Via Parigi 5 ☎ 06 488 991 ⓞ Mon–Sat 8am–7pm
● Information kiosks (daily 9–6) are at ✉ Largo Goldoni ☎ 06 6813 6061; ✉ Piazza Tempio della Pace ☎ 06 6992 4307; ✉ Piazza delle Cinque Lune ☎ 06 6880 9240; ✉ Palazzo delle Esposizioni, Via Nazionale ☎ 06 4782 4525; ✉ Piazza San Giovanni in Laterano ☎ 06 7720 3535; ✉ Lungotevere Castel Sant'Angelo-Piazza Pia ☎ 06 6880 9707

MEDICAL TREATMENT

There are emergency rooms at these centres: Ospedale Fatebenefratelli ✉ Isola Tiberina ☎ 06 683 7299/06 68371; Policlinico Umberto I ✉ Viale del Policlinico 155 ☎ 06 446 2341 or 06 49971; www.policlinicoumberto1.it. The George Eastman Clinic (✉ Viale Regina Elena 287/b ☎ 06 844 831) provides an emergency dentist service. No credit cards.

Pharmacies are indicated by a large green cross. Opening times are usually Mon–Sat 8.30–1, 4–8, but a rotating schedule (displayed on pharmacy doors) ensures at least one is open 24 hours a day, seven days a week. The most central English-speaking pharmacist is Internazionale (✉ Piazza Barberini 49 ☎ 06 482 5456).

EMERGENCY NUMBERS

Police, Fire and Ambulance (general SOS) ☎ 113
Police (Carabinieri) ☎ 112
Central Police ☎ 06 46861
UK Embassy ☎ 06 4220 0001
US Embassy ☎ 06 46741
Information ☎ 12
International information (Europe) ☎ 176
International information (rest of the world) ☎ 170
ACI Auto Assistance (car breakdowns) ☎ 116
General info-tourist line ☎ 06 8205 9127

Language

All Italian words are pronounced as written, with each vowel and consonant sounded. Only the letter *h* is silent, but it modifies the sound of other letters. The letter *c* is hard, as in English 'cat', except when followed by *i* or *e*, when it becomes the soft *ch* of 'cello'. Similarly, *g* is soft (as in the English 'giant') when followed by *i* or *e*–*giardino*, *gelati*; otherwise hard (as in 'gas')–*gatto*. Words ending in *o* are almost always masculine in gender (plural: *-i*); those ending in *a* are generally feminine (plural: *-e*). Use the polite second person (*lei*) to speak to strangers and the informal second person (*tu*) to friends or children.

USEFUL WORDS

yes	*sì*
no	*no*
please	*per piacere*
thank you	*grazie*
you're welcome	*prego*
excuse me! !	*scusi*
where	*dove*
here	*qui*
there	*là*
when	*quando*
now	*adesso*
later	*più tardi*
why	*perchè*
who	*chi*
may I/can I	*posso*
good morning	*buon giorno*
good afternoon	*buona sera*
good evening	*buona notte*
hello/good-bye (informal)	*ciao*
hello (on the telephone)	*pronto*
I'm sorry	*mi dispiace*
left/right	*sinistra/destra*
open/closed	*aperto/chiuso*
good/bad	*buono/cattivo*
big/small	*grande/piccolo*
with/without	*con/senza*
more/less	*più/meno*
hot/cold	*caldo/freddo*
early/late	*presto/ritardo*
now/later	*adesso/più tardi*
today/tomorrow	*oggi/domani*
when?/do you have?	*quando?/avete?*

NUMBERS

1	*uno, una*
2	*due*
3	*tre*
4	*quattro*
5	*cinque*
6	*sei*
7	*sette*
8	*otto*
9	*nove*
10	*dieci*
20	*venti*
30	*trenta*
40	*quaranta*
50	*cinquanta*
100	*cento*
1,000	*mille*

EMERGENCIES

help!	*aiuto!*
stop, thief!	*al ladro!*
can you help me, please?	*può aiutarmi, per favore?*
call the police/an ambulance	*chiami la polizia/un'ambulanza*
I have lost my wallet/passport	*ho perso il mio portafoglio/il mio passaporto*
where is the police station?	*dov'è il commissariato?*
where is the hospital?	*dov'è l'ospedale?*
I don't feel well	*non mi sento bene*
first aid	*pronto soccorso*

COLOURS

black	*nero*
brown	*marrone*
pink	*rosa*
red	*rosso*
orange	*arancia*
yellow	*giallo*
green	*verde*
light blue	*celeste*
sky blue	*azzuro*
purple	*viola*
white	*bianco*
grey	*grigio*

USEFUL PHRASES

how are you? (informal)	*come sta/stai?*
I'm fine	*sto bene*
I do not understand	*non ho capito*
how much is it?	*quant'è?*
do you have a room?	*avete camere libere?*
how much per night?	*quanto costa una notte?*
with bath/shower	*con vasca/doccia*
when is breakfast served?	*a che ora è servita la colazione?*
where is the train/bus station?	*dov'è la stazione ferroviaria degli autobus?*
where are we?	*dove siamo?*
do I have to get off here?	*devo scendere qui?*
I'm looking for...	*cerco...*
where can I buy...?	*dove posso comprare...?*
a table for... please	*un tavolo per... per favore*
the bill, please?	*il conto, per favore*
we didn't have this	*non abbiamo avuto questo*
where are the toilets?	*dove sono i bagni?*

DAYS/MONTHS

Monday	*lunedì*
Tuesday	*martedì*
Wednesday	*mercoledì*
Thursday	*giovedì*
Friday	*venerdì*
Saturday	*sabato*
Sunday	*domenica*
January	*gennaio*
February	*febbraio*
March	*marzo*
April	*aprile*
May	*maggio*
June	*giugno*
July	*luglio*
August	*agosto*
September	*settembre*
October	*ottobre*
November	*novembre*
December	*dicembre*

Timeline

PUNIC WARS

The First Punic War against Carthage (North Africa) started in 264BC and lasted for around 23 years. In the Second Punic War (218–201BC) Rome was threatened by Hannibal, leader of the Carthaginian army. But Rome finally defeated Carthage in the Third Punic War (149–146BC).

RELIGION

There are 280 churches within the city walls and 94 per cent of Romans have had their children baptized. However, only 23 per cent of Romans attend Mass. Forty per cent of Romans favour women priests.

Caius Julius Caesar (left); map of the Roman Empire (middle); Charlemagne— his coronation as Holy Roman Emperor (right)

753BC Traditional date of the foundation of Rome by Romulus, first of the city's seven kings.

616–578BC Tarquinius Priscus, Rome's first Etruscan king.

509BC Etruscans expelled and the Republic founded.

60BC Rome ruled by a triumvirate of Pompey, Marcus Licinius Crassus and Caesar.

48BC Caesar declared ruler for life but assassinated by rivals in 44BC.

27BC–AD14 Rule of Octavian, Caesar's great nephew, who as Augustus becomes the first Roman emperor.

98–117 Reign of Emperor Trajan. Military campaigns extend the Empire's boundaries.

284–286 Empire divided into East and West.

306–337 The Emperor Constantine reunites the Empire legalising Christianity. St. Peter's and the first Christian churches are built.

410 Rome is sacked by the Goths.

476 Romulus Augustulus is the last Roman Emperor.

800 Charlemagne awards some territories to

papacy; Pope Leo III crowns him Holy Roman Emperor.

1508 Michelangelo begins the Sistine Chapel ceiling.

1527 Rome is sacked by German and Spanish troops under Charles V.

1848 Uprisings in Rome under Mazzini and Garibaldi force Pope Pius IX to flee. The new 'Roman Republic' is defeated by the French.

1870 Rome joins a united Italy.

1929 The Lateran Treaty recognizes the Vatican as a separate state.

1940 Italy enters World War II.

1960 Rome hosts the Olympic Games.

2000 Some 30 million pilgrims visit Rome for the millennial jubilee year.

2005 Pope John Paul II dies and is succeeded by Pope Benedict XVI.

2006 Romano Prodi of the centre left party-takes the Italian presidency from Silvio Berlusconi in April elections.

2008 Berlusconi is reelected after the collapse of the government. Gianni Alemanno is elected Rome's first right-wing Mayor since WWII.

WHAT'S IN A NAME

Many of Rome's street names include dates that allude to significant events in the city's history. Via XX Settembre (20 September) remembers that day in 1870 when Italian troops liberated Rome: the city became the city's capital in the same year. Via XXIV Maggio (24 May) recalls the day in 1915 that Italy declared war in 1915 during World War I. Via IV Novembre (4 November) alludes to the date of the Italian armistice and victory in 1918 after World War I. And Via XXV Aprile (25 April) commemorates the day in 1944 that the Allies liberated the city from the Nazi rule.

Gladiators at a Funeral (left); Charlemagne et ses ecoliers (middle); Garibaldi, a popular leader (right)

Index

Rome's
25 Best

WRITTEN BY Tim Jepson
UPDATED BY Adele Evans
DESIGN WORK Jacqueline Bailey
COVER DESIGN Tigist Getachew
INDEXER Marie Lorimer
IMAGE RETOUCHING AND REPRO Michael Moody, Sarah Montgomery
EDITORIAL MANAGEMENT Apostrophe S Limited
REVIEWING EDITOR Linda Cabasin
SERIES EDITOR Marie-Claire Jefferies

ISBN 978-1-4000-0383-9

EIGHTH EDITION

IMPORTANT TIP
Time inevitably brings changes, so always confirm prices, travel facts, and other perishable information when it matters. Although Fodor's cannot accept responsibility for errors, you can use this guide in the confidence that we have taken every care to ensure its accuracy.

SPECIAL SALES
This book is available for special discounts for bulk purchases for sales promotions or premiums. Special editions, including personalized covers, excerpts of existing books, and corporate imprints, can be created in large quantities for special needs. For more information, write to Special Markets/Premium Sales, 1745 Broadway, MD 6–2, New York, NY 10019 or email specialmarkets@randomhouse.com.

Color separation by Keenes, Andover, UK
Printed and bound by Leo Paper Products, China
10 9 8 7 6 5 4 3 2

A04461
Mapping in this title produced from mapping © MAIRDUMONT / Falk Verlag 2010.
Transport map © Communicarta Ltd, UK

The Automobile Association wishes to thank the following photographers, companies and picture libraries for their assistance in the preparation of this book.

Abbreviations for the picture credits are as follows – (t) top; (b) bottom; (l) left; (r) right; (c) center; (AA) AA World Travel Library

1 AA/C Sawyer; 2 AA/A Kouprianoff; 3 AA/A Kouprianoff; 4t AA/A Kouprianoff; 4c AA/S McBride; 5t AA/A Kouprianoff; 5c AA/D Miterdiri; 6t AA/A Kouprianoff; 6cl AA/C Sawyer; 6c AA/S McBride; 6cr AA/S McBride; 6bl AA/C Sawyer; 6cbl AA/C Sawyer; 6bc AA/S McBride; 6br AA/A Kouprianoff; 7t AA/A Kouprianoff; 7cl AA/S McBride; 7c AA/S McBride; 7cr AA/S McBride; 7bl AA/S McBride; 7bc AA/S McBride; 7br AA/S McBride; 8 AA/A Kouprianoff; 9 AA/A Kouprianoff; 10t AA/A Kouprianoff; 10ct AA/S McBride; 10c AA/S McBride; 10cb AA/C Sawyer; 10/11 AA/S McBride; 11t AA/A Kouprianoff; 11ct AA/A Kouprianoff; 11c AA/C Sawyer; 12t AA/A Kouprianoff; 12b AA/C Sawyer; 13t AA/A Kouprianoff; 13tct AA/A Kouprianoff; 13ct AA/D Miterdiri; 13c AA/A Kouprianoff; 13cb AA; 13b AA/S McBride; 14t AA/A Kouprianoff; 14ct AA/C Sawyer; 14c AA/J Holmes; 14cb AA/M Jourdan; 14b AA/C Sawyer; 15 AA/A Kouprianoff; 16t AA/A Kouprianoff; 16ct AA/A Kouprianoff; 16c AA/C Sawyer; 16cb AA/A Kouprianoff; 16b AA/D Miterdiri; 17t AA/A Kouprianoff; 17ct Digital Vision; 17c AA/C Sawyer; 17cb AA/C Sawyer; 17b AA/S McBride; 18t AA/A Kouprianoff; 18ct AA/P Wilson; 18c AA/A Kouprianoff; 18cb AA/C Sawyer; 18b AA/S McBride; 19i AA/A Kouprianoff; 19ii AA/J Holmes; 19iii AA/J Holmes; 19iv AA/S McBride; 19v AA/J Holmes; 19vi AA/T Souter; 20/21 AA/A Kouprianoff; 24l AA/J Holmes; 24/25 AA/S McBride; 24c AA/C Sawyer; 24tr AA/A Kouprianoff; 24cl AA/S McBride; 25cr AA/A Kouprianoff; 26l AA/A Kouprianoff; 26/27 AA/C Sawyer; 26c AA/P Wilson; 27c AA/P Wilson; 27r AA/S McBride; 28l AA/C Sawyer; 28/29 AA/S McBride; 28/29b AA/J Holmes; 29tr AA/S McBride; 29cl AA/C Sawyer; 29cr AA/C Sawyer; 30l AA/S McBride; 30r AA/J Holmes; 31l AA/S McBride; 31r AA/M Jourdan; 32l AA/D Miterdiri; 32r AA/S McBride; 33t AA/D Miterdiri; 33bl AA/T Souter; 33br AA/S McBride; 34t AA/D Miterdiri; 34bl AA/S McBride; 34br AA/P Wilson; 35t AA/D Miterdiri; 35bl AA/A Kouprianoff; 35br AA/D Miterdiri; 36 AA/J Holmes; 37t AA/C Saywer; 37c AA/S McBride; 38 AA/J Holmes; 39 AA/A Kouprianoff; 40l Alamy/Pieter Estersohn; 42/43t AA/S McBride; 42/43b AA/S McBride; 43 Alamy/CuboImages srl; 44 AA/J Holmes; 44/45 AA/P Wilson; 46l AA/S McBride; 46tr AA/S McBride; 46/47 AA/S McBride; 47t AA/S McBride; 47bl AA/S McBride; 47br AA/S McBride; 48l AA/C Sawyer; 48c AA/C Sawyer; 48r AA/C Sawyer; 49l AA/C Sawyer; 49r AA/P Wilson; 50l AA/C Sawyer; 50c AA; 50r AA/C Sawyer; 51t AA/D Miterdiri; 51bl AA/C Sawyer; 51br AA/J Holmes; 52t AA/D Miterdiri; 52bl AA/C Sawyer; 52br AA/J Holmes; 53 AA/D Miterdiri; 54 AA/C Sawyer; 55 AA/P Wilson; 56 AA/C Sawyer; 57 AA/A Kouprianoff; 58 AA/C Sawyer; 59 AA/C Sawyer; 60 AA/C Sawyer; 61 AA/A Kouprianoff; 64l AA/A Kouprianoff; 64tr AA/S McBride; 64/65 AA/S McBride; 65t AA/D Miterdiri; 65cl AA/S McBride; 65cr AA/S McBride; 66l AA/D Miterdiri; 66r AA/A Kouprianoff; 67t AA/D Miterdiri; 67bl AA/S McBride; 67br AA/S McBride; 68t AA/D Miterdiri; 68bl AA/J Holmes; 68br AA/J Holmes; 69t AA/D Miterdiri; 69bl AA/S McBride; 69br AA/J Holmes; 70 AA/D Miterdiri; 71 AA/M Chaplow; 72 Digital Vision; 73 Brand X Pictures; 74 AA/T Harris; 75 AA/C Sawyer; 78l AA/S McBride; 78c AA/S McBride; 78r AA/S McBride; 79l AA/P Wilson; 79r AA/D Miterdiri; 80l AA/P Wilson; 80r AA/P Wilson; 81l AA/C Sawyer; 81c AA/J Holmes; 81r AA/C Sawyer; 82 AA/S McBride; 82/83 Alamy/Rough Guides; 84l AA/J Holmes; 84r AA/J Holmes; 85l AA/D Miterdiri; 85r Alamy/Peter Horree; 86t AA/D Miterdiri; 86bl AA; 86br AA/D Miterdiri; 87t AA/D Miterdiri; 87bl AA/D Miterdiri; 87br AA/P Wilson; 88 AA/D Miterdiri; 89 Photodisc; 90t Digital Vision; 90c AA/E Meacher; 91 AA/J Holmes; 94l AA/S McBride; 94r AA/S McBride; 95l AA/C Sawyer; 95r AA/S McBride; 96l AA/S McBride; 96tr AA/S McBride; 96cr AA/S McBride; 97t AA/S McBride; 97cl AA/S McBride; 97cr AA/S McBride; 98t AA/S McBride; 98c AA/C Sawyer; 99 AA/S McBride; 102t AA/S McBride; 102cl AA/Marshall Ikonography/Alamy; 102cr AA/C Saywer; 103t AA/S McBride; 103cl AA/C Sawyer; 103cr AA/C Sawyer; 104t AA/D Miterdiri; 104bl AA/S McBride; 104br AA/J Holmes; 105t AA/S McBride; 105bl AA/S McBride; 105bc AA/S McBride; 105br AA/S McBride; 106t Photodisc; 106c AA/C Sawyer; 107 AA/P Wilson; 108t AA/C Sawyer; 108ct Photodisc; 108c AA/C Sawyer; 108cb AA/C Sawyer; 108b AA; 109 AA/C Sawyer; 110 AA/C Sawyer; 111 AA/C Sawyer; 112 AA/C Sawyer; 113 AA/J Holmes; 114 AA/S McBride; 115 AA/S McBride; 116 AA/S McBride; 117 AA/S McBride; 118 AA/S McBride; 119 AA/S McBride; 120 AA/S McBride; 120 European Central Bank; 121 AA/S McBride; 122t AA/S McBride; 122b AA/J Holmes; 123 AA/S McBride; 124t AA/S McBride; 124bl AA; 124bc AA; 124br AA; 125t AA/S McBride; 125bl AA; 125bc AA; 125br AA